HOW IT WORKS
THE
WORLD OF
FLIGHT

Text by Bill Gunston

Illustrated by Ian Howatson and Sebastian Quigley

HORUS EDITIONS

ISBN 1-899762-36-1

Copyright © 1995 Horus Editions Limited

First published 1995
This edition first published 1997
Fourth impression 2000

Published by Horus Editions Limited,
1st floor, 27 Longford Street,
London NW1 3DZ

Printed in Singapore

HOW IT WORKS

CONTENTS

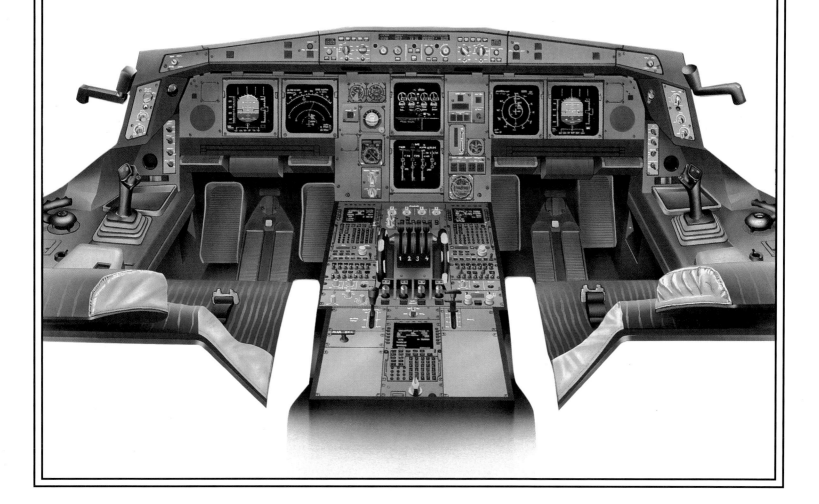

Balloons

JUST over 200 years ago, in 1783, two Frenchmen, Joseph and Etienne Montgolfier, discovered that hot air rises. This is because hot air has a lower density than cold air. The hot, lower density air inside a hot-air balloon makes the balloon lighter. The cooler, higher density air around it forces the balloon to rise. Thousands of people enjoy going up in hot-air balloons. They stand in a strong but light basket. The basket also carries liquid fuel, called propane, which feeds a burner. The burner is used to send a long flame into the balloon to heat the air inside. The balloon floats along, carried by the wind. Every now and then the air inside has to be heated up again by switching on the burner. If the balloon's air is not reheated, the balloon and basket will begin to descend.

THE BRAZIER

WHEN THE AERONAUT (PILOT) PULLS ON A HANDLE, FUEL IS FED TO THE BURNER, CAUSING A HUGE FLAME

Montgolfier
In 1783 the Montgolfier balloon (*above*) carried the first people on any kind of air flight. Cords supported the wickerwork gallery at the bottom, and chains carried the brazier under the envelope. The Montgolfier brothers did not realize it was the hot air from the brazier that made it fly; they thought they had invented a new gas.

Hydrogen balloon
Pictured left is one of the first balloons to be filled with a low-density gas, instead of hot air. Hydrogen is the lightest of all gases, so it gives the most powerful lift. Unlike a hot-air balloon, a hydrogen balloon does not need a burner. Over 200 years ago people travelled in hydrogen balloons.

THE BASKET IS MADE OF STRONG WICKERWORK

HANDHOLDS ARE USED TO HOLD THE BALLOON STEADY JUST BEFORE LIFTOFF AND AFTER LANDING

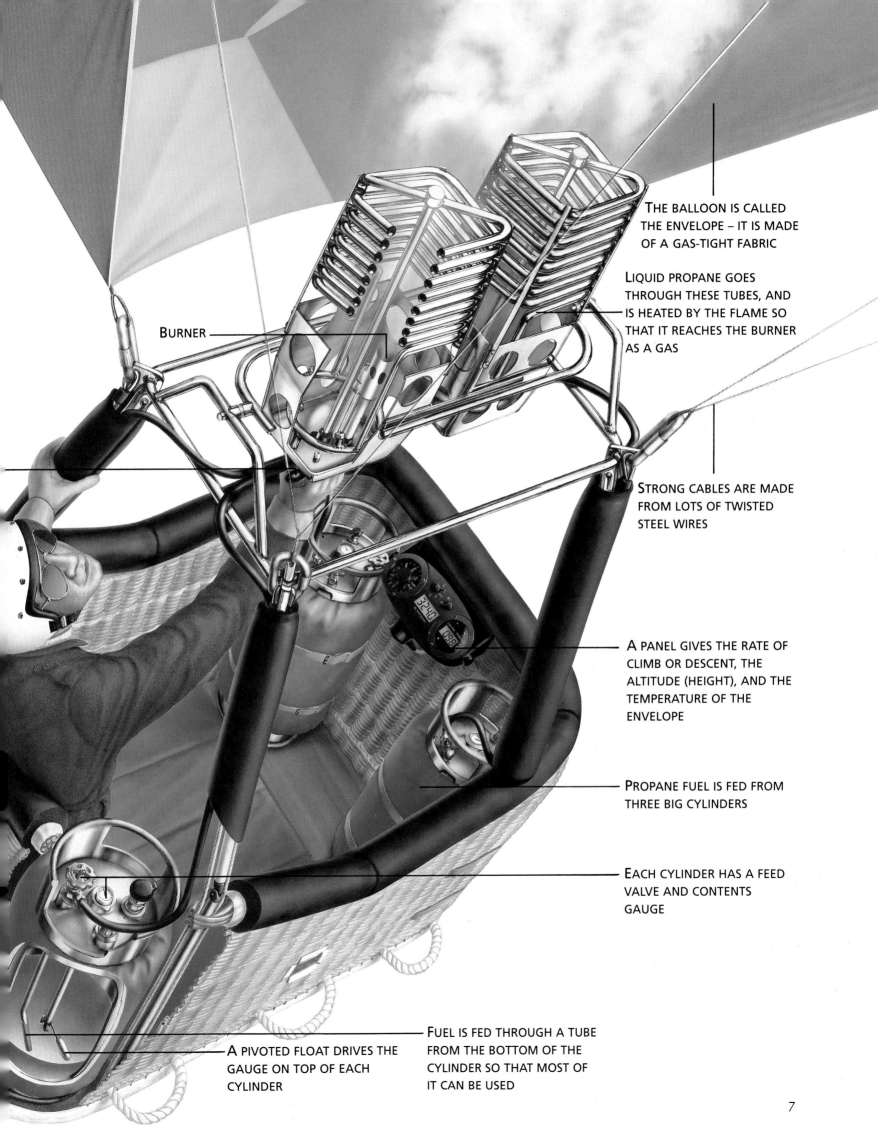

THE BALLOON IS CALLED THE ENVELOPE – IT IS MADE OF A GAS-TIGHT FABRIC

LIQUID PROPANE GOES THROUGH THESE TUBES, AND IS HEATED BY THE FLAME SO THAT IT REACHES THE BURNER AS A GAS

BURNER

STRONG CABLES ARE MADE FROM LOTS OF TWISTED STEEL WIRES

A PANEL GIVES THE RATE OF CLIMB OR DESCENT, THE ALTITUDE (HEIGHT), AND THE TEMPERATURE OF THE ENVELOPE

PROPANE FUEL IS FED FROM THREE BIG CYLINDERS

EACH CYLINDER HAS A FEED VALVE AND CONTENTS GAUGE

A PIVOTED FLOAT DRIVES THE GAUGE ON TOP OF EACH CYLINDER

FUEL IS FED THROUGH A TUBE FROM THE BOTTOM OF THE CYLINDER SO THAT MOST OF IT CAN BE USED

Airships

BALLOONS are blown wherever the wind takes them. For going in chosen directions the airship was invented. Early airships had an envelope with a rigid frame, containing separate gas bags. Today, airships are non-rigids, which means they have an envelope made of flexible fabric, like a balloon. Helium fills most of the envelope. Helium is a gas which is less dense and therefore lighter than air, so it lifts the airship. The gondola, or cabin, of a modern, non-rigid airship (*right*) carries two piston engines, which drive propellers that lie inside ducts. The ducts can be swivelled round to make the propellers push the airship forward, up, or down.

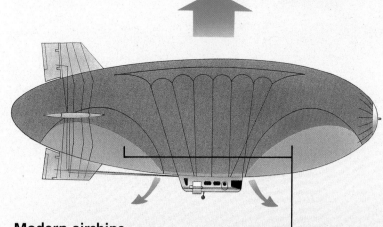

Modern airships
Most of the envelope contains helium, which lifts the weight of the airship. But two large bags, called ballonets, contain air. For the airship to rise or fall, air is pumped out (*above*), or in (*above right*).

AIR BAGS, CALLED BALLONETS, LIE AT THE FRONT AND BACK OF THE AIRSHIP

THESE FLAP VALVES CONTROL THE AIRFLOW TO THE AFT BALLONET

An early airship
In 1852 a Frenchman called Henri Giffard made the first airship (*below*). The envelope was long and pointed instead of round, like a balloon's. Underneath hung a container that had a seat and small steam engine which drove a propeller. Early airships had such weak engines they could fly only on very calm days.

CABLES SUPPORT THE GONDOLA OF THIS MODERN AIRSHIP

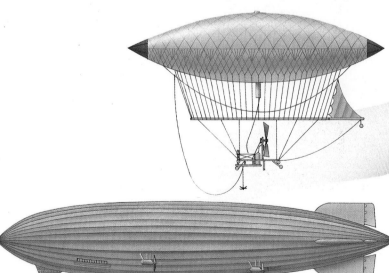

THIS TUBE FEEDS AIR TO THE AFT (REAR) BALLONET TO CONTROL THE SHIP

THE DOOR TO THE ENGINE ROOM

THIS PULLEY ALLOWS THE PILOT TO CONTROL THE RUDDERS AND STEER THE AIRSHIP

LZ 129 Hindenburg
The greatest airship was built in 1935 (*above*). Named the *Hindenburg*, it was a rigid airship and had 25 double bedrooms for passengers. This hydrogen-filled airship burst into flames in 1937.

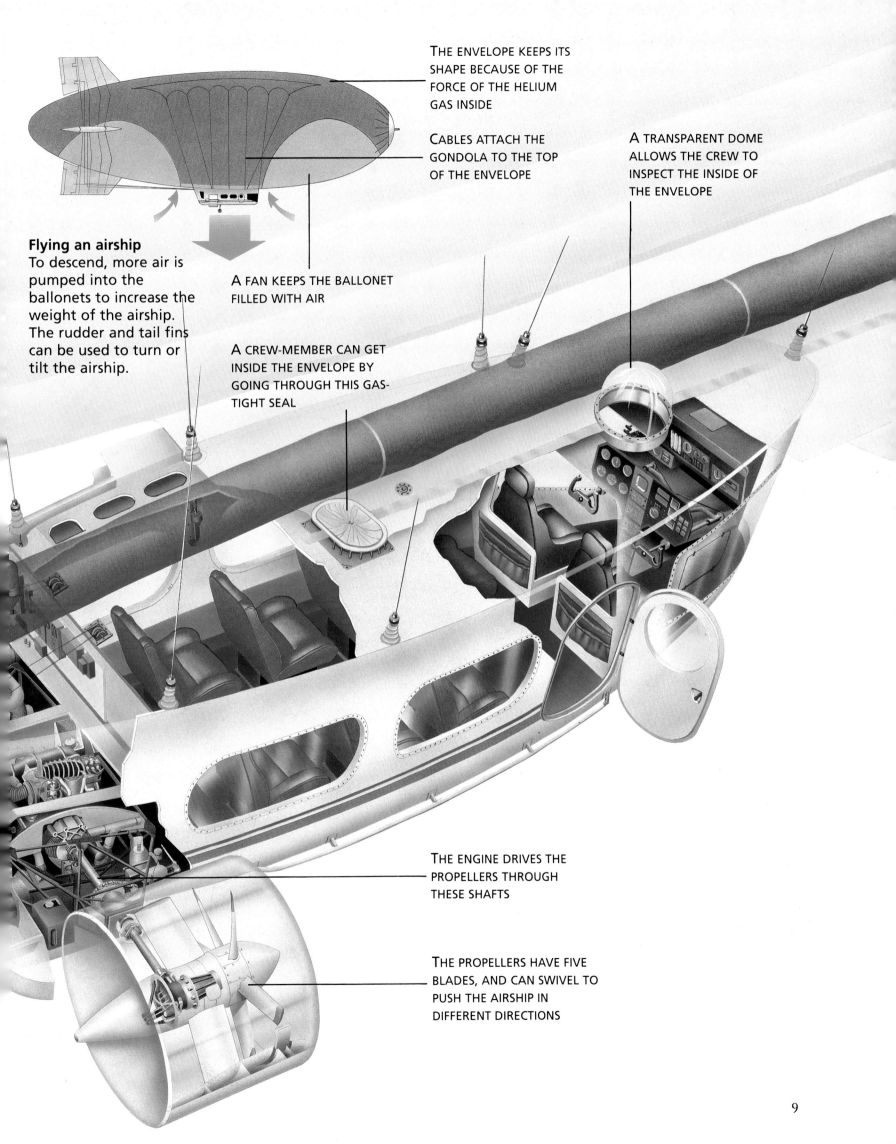

THE ENVELOPE KEEPS ITS SHAPE BECAUSE OF THE FORCE OF THE HELIUM GAS INSIDE

CABLES ATTACH THE GONDOLA TO THE TOP OF THE ENVELOPE

A TRANSPARENT DOME ALLOWS THE CREW TO INSPECT THE INSIDE OF THE ENVELOPE

Flying an airship
To descend, more air is pumped into the ballonets to increase the weight of the airship. The rudder and tail fins can be used to turn or tilt the airship.

A FAN KEEPS THE BALLONET FILLED WITH AIR

A CREW-MEMBER CAN GET INSIDE THE ENVELOPE BY GOING THROUGH THIS GAS-TIGHT SEAL

THE ENGINE DRIVES THE PROPELLERS THROUGH THESE SHAFTS

THE PROPELLERS HAVE FIVE BLADES, AND CAN SWIVEL TO PUSH THE AIRSHIP IN DIFFERENT DIRECTIONS

The First Aeroplane

THE first successful aeroplane, called the *Flyer*, was made by American brothers, Wilbur and Orville Wright. They started by flying gliders. These were biplanes, with two sets of wings. They then added a horizontal tail at the front to act as elevators. Elevators are used to make an aeroplane climb and dive. Two rudders in the vertical tail at the back were used to steer the *Flyer*. To hold the wings level, or to roll the *Flyer* to the left or right, wires were added for twisting the wings. Next they made a 12-horsepower engine and used bicycle chains to turn two big 'pusher' propellers. The pilot controlled the *Flyer* with two levers and by shifting his body to the left or right.

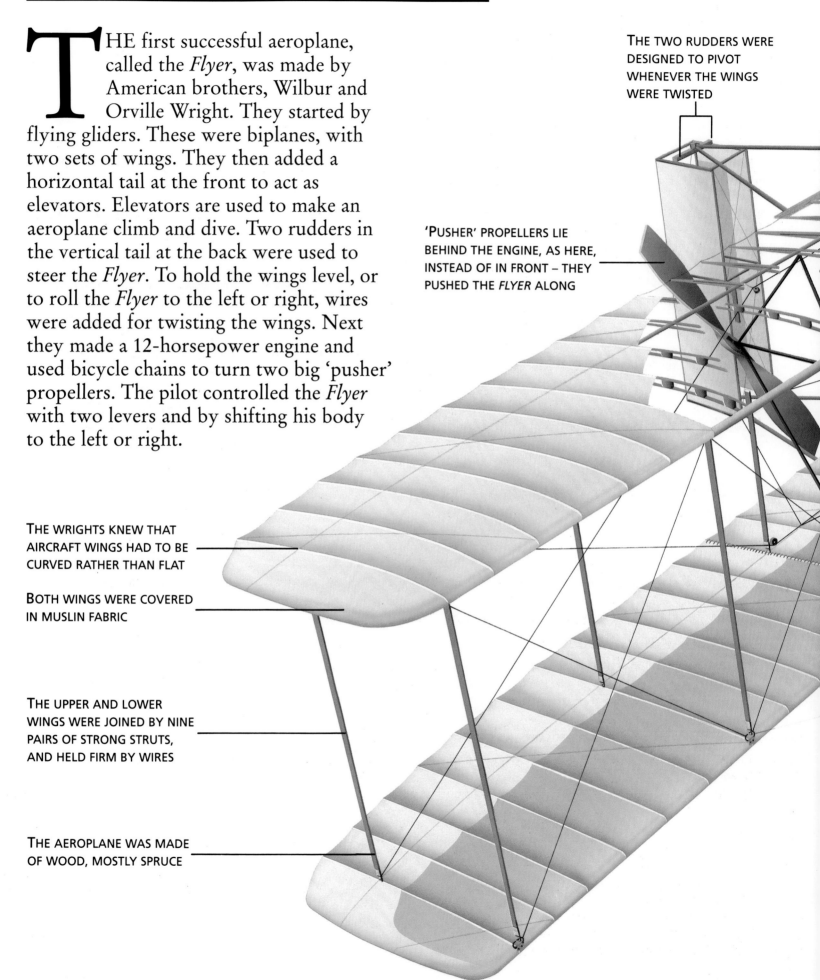

THE TWO RUDDERS WERE DESIGNED TO PIVOT WHENEVER THE WINGS WERE TWISTED

'PUSHER' PROPELLERS LIE BEHIND THE ENGINE, AS HERE, INSTEAD OF IN FRONT – THEY PUSHED THE *FLYER* ALONG

THE WRIGHTS KNEW THAT AIRCRAFT WINGS HAD TO BE CURVED RATHER THAN FLAT

BOTH WINGS WERE COVERED IN MUSLIN FABRIC

THE UPPER AND LOWER WINGS WERE JOINED BY NINE PAIRS OF STRONG STRUTS, AND HELD FIRM BY WIRES

THE AEROPLANE WAS MADE OF WOOD, MOSTLY SPRUCE

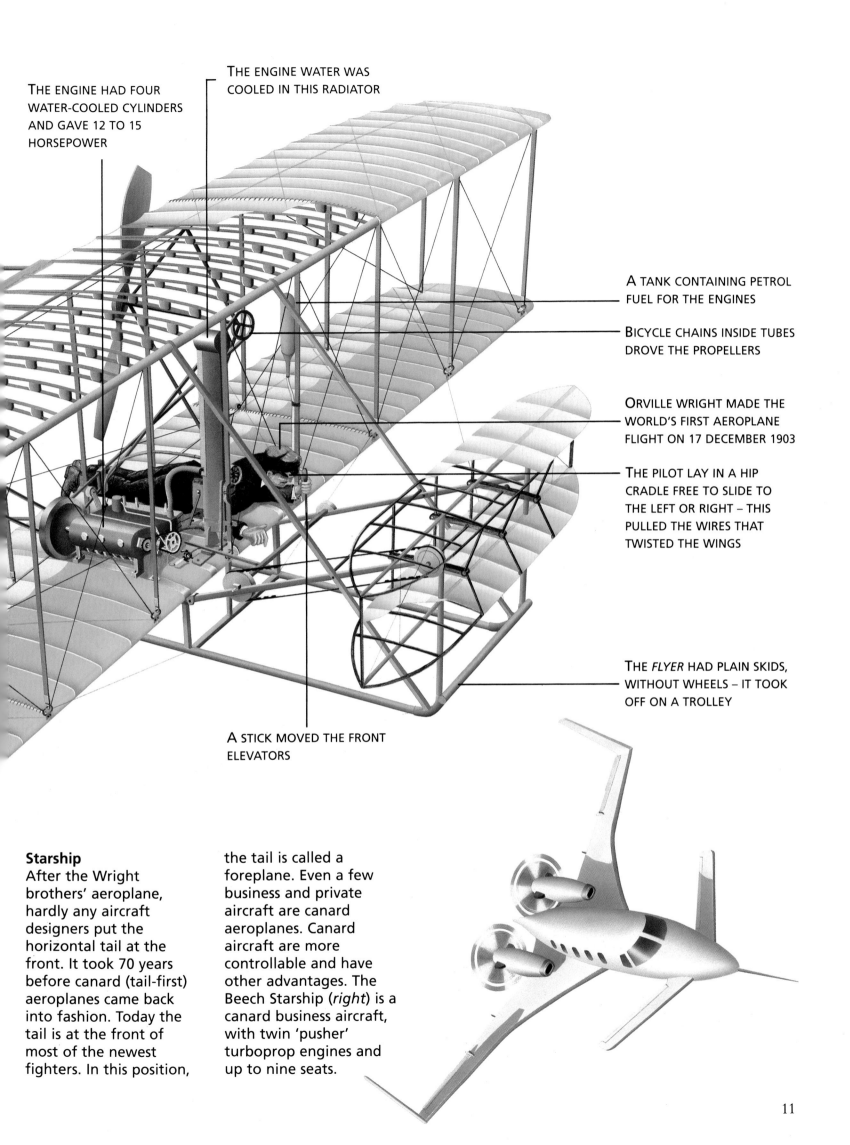

THE ENGINE HAD FOUR WATER-COOLED CYLINDERS AND GAVE 12 TO 15 HORSEPOWER

THE ENGINE WATER WAS COOLED IN THIS RADIATOR

A TANK CONTAINING PETROL FUEL FOR THE ENGINES

BICYCLE CHAINS INSIDE TUBES DROVE THE PROPELLERS

ORVILLE WRIGHT MADE THE WORLD'S FIRST AEROPLANE FLIGHT ON 17 DECEMBER 1903

THE PILOT LAY IN A HIP CRADLE FREE TO SLIDE TO THE LEFT OR RIGHT – THIS PULLED THE WIRES THAT TWISTED THE WINGS

THE *FLYER* HAD PLAIN SKIDS, WITHOUT WHEELS – IT TOOK OFF ON A TROLLEY

A STICK MOVED THE FRONT ELEVATORS

Starship

After the Wright brothers' aeroplane, hardly any aircraft designers put the horizontal tail at the front. It took 70 years before canard (tail-first) aeroplanes came back into fashion. Today the tail is at the front of most of the newest fighters. In this position, the tail is called a foreplane. Even a few business and private aircraft are canard aeroplanes. Canard aircraft are more controllable and have other advantages. The Beech Starship (*right*) is a canard business aircraft, with twin 'pusher' turboprop engines and up to nine seats.

11

Early Aeroplanes

BEFORE 1930 most aeroplanes were made of wood or steel tubes, or both. They were almost always held firm with wires and covered with flimsy fabric. Designers then began to make aeroplanes entirely out of metal. Their strong metal skins, or outer layer, could withstand the pushes, pulls, and twists of flight. This meant designers could do away with wires and struts. Next, retractable landing gear was added, so the wheels could be folded away inside the aeroplane.

1915 All-metal aircraft
Apart from an unsuccessful machine of 1910, this German monoplane of December 1915 was the first all-metal aircraft. It was made of steel sheets, protected by a thin layer of tin.

JUNKERS J1

1939 Jet aeroplane
First flown on 27 August 1939, the Heinkel He 178 was the first jet aeroplane in the world. It was powered by a turbojet engine, invented by a German, Pabst von Ohain. An Englishman, Frank Whittle, had invented the same kind of engine seven years earlier. But when Whittle said that he had, no one believed him!

HEINKEL He 178

1951 Swept-back wings
Engineers discovered that a fast jet can go even faster if its wings are swept back. The Bell X-5 was first flown in America in 1951. Its wings could be pivoted from 20 to 60 degrees during flight. Today wings of many fast jets can do this.

BELL X-5

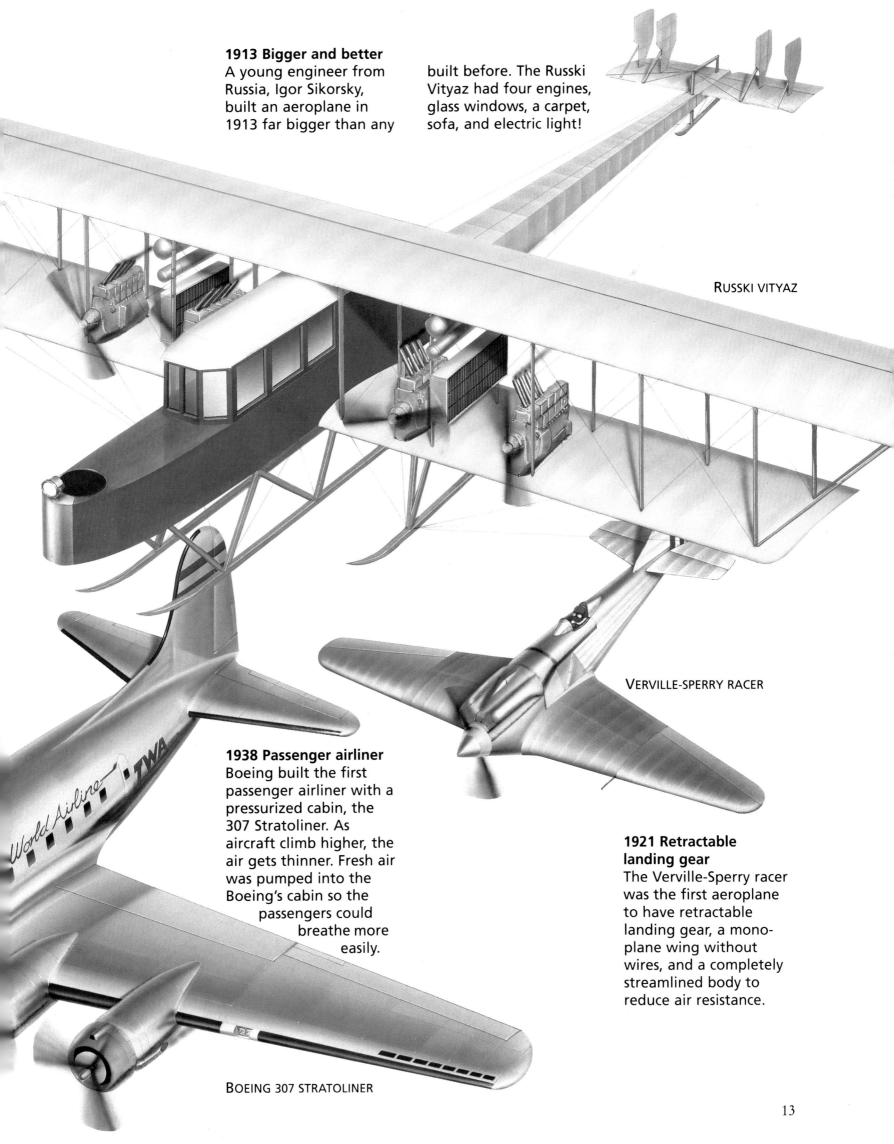

1913 Bigger and better

A young engineer from Russia, Igor Sikorsky, built an aeroplane in 1913 far bigger than any built before. The Russki Vityaz had four engines, glass windows, a carpet, sofa, and electric light!

RUSSKI VITYAZ

VERVILLE-SPERRY RACER

1938 Passenger airliner

Boeing built the first passenger airliner with a pressurized cabin, the 307 Stratoliner. As aircraft climb higher, the air gets thinner. Fresh air was pumped into the Boeing's cabin so the passengers could breathe more easily.

1921 Retractable landing gear

The Verville-Sperry racer was the first aeroplane to have retractable landing gear, a monoplane wing without wires, and a completely streamlined body to reduce air resistance.

BOEING 307 STRATOLINER

How Aeroplanes Fly

FOR an aeroplane to fly, it must have one or more fixed wings, a propulsion system (propeller or jet), and flight controls to guide it. To stop an aeroplane from being pulled down to earth by its own weight, a force called lift must be created. To do this an aeroplane must move along fast, and its wings must be a special cambered, or curved, shape (*see right*).

The whole body of an aeroplane must have a stream-lined, or smooth, shape so air can pass freely around it. A shape that is not streamlined would cause greater friction with the air, known as drag, and hold the aeroplane back too much.

Lift
The upward force caused by a wing moving through the air is called lift. Almost all lift is produced by the air that passes across the top of the wing. This air has to speed up and rush over the wing much faster than the air passing underneath. Speeding up the air greatly reduces its pressure, so that it sucks the wing upwards.

THE FIN IS LIKE THE FEATHERS ON A DART OR ARROW – IT KEEPS THE AIRCRAFT POINTING THE RIGHT WAY

FRICTION WITH THE AIR CAUSES DRAG, WHICH TRIES TO HOLD THE AIRCRAFT BACK

DOWN-LOAD, OR WEIGHT, ON THE TAILPLANE KEEPS THE AIRCRAFT BALANCED

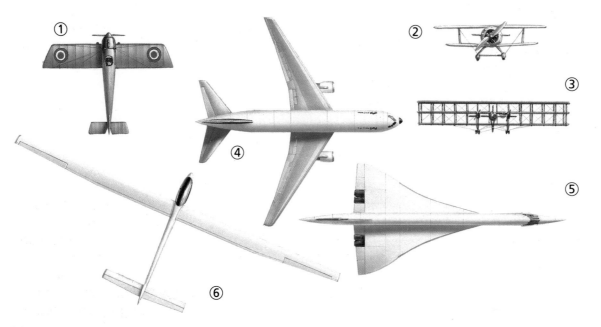

Aeroplane shapes
(1) is a monoplane (with one set of wings) fighter of 1915. (2) is a biplane (two sets of wings). (3) is a triplane (three sets of wings) bomber of 1915. (4) is a big modern jetliner, with two engines. (5) is the distinctive Concorde supersonic airliner. (6) is a glider, with long slender wings to help it stay up without an engine.

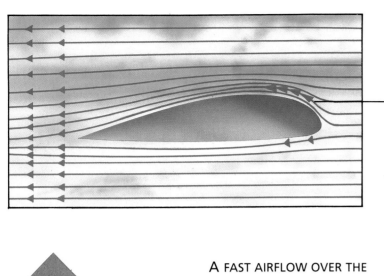

THE AIR RUSHING OVER THE WING HAS A LOWER PRESSURE

Wings
It is easy to see what wings look like from above, but it is just as important to see what they look like in cross-section. The shape is called an aerofoil.

A FAST AIRFLOW OVER THE TOP OF THE WING CAUSES LIFT

PROPELLERS ARE THE PROPULSION SYSTEM WHICH PROPELS, OR DRIVES, THE AIRCRAFT FORWARDS

THE AIRCRAFT IS PROPELLED FORWARDS

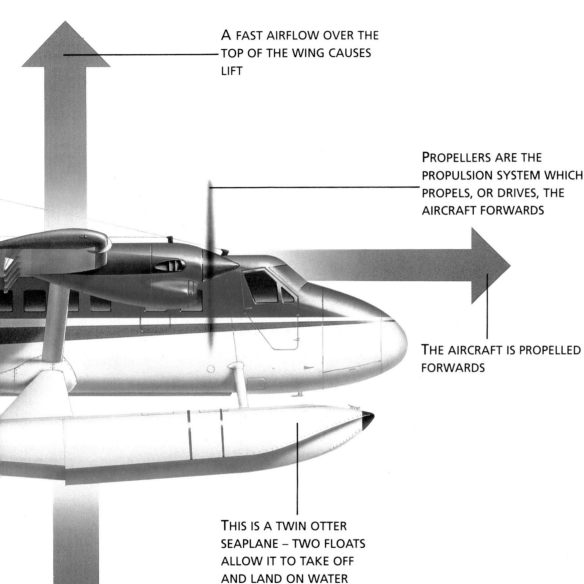

THIS IS A TWIN OTTER SEAPLANE – TWO FLOATS ALLOW IT TO TAKE OFF AND LAND ON WATER

WITHOUT LIFT, THE WEIGHT OF THE AIRCRAFT WOULD PULL IT DOWN TO EARTH

About 100 years ago wings were just flat sheets set at an angle.

The Wright brothers made their wings cambered (curved).

Heavy bombers in World War II had thick metal wings, able to lift well at low speeds.

Early jet airliners had thinner wings, with slats and powerful flaps.

The latest jet airliners have 'supercritical' wings, flatter on top and bulged underneath (which stops the air above the wing from speeding up too much).

15

The Controls

INSIDE the Boeing 747 or 'Jumbo Jet' there are more than 5,000 sets of controls. Pilots control the aeroplane with the help of a system of hinged parts, called control surfaces. They are driven by powerful hydraulic jacks. From the cockpit, the pilot sends out commands through a mechanical system of cables to make the hydraulic jacks push, pull, and rotate the surfaces. The control surfaces include: ailerons (for roll); elevators (for climb and dive); rudder (for direction); spoilers (for roll, and to act as airbrakes); leading-edge slats or flaps (for extra lift at low speeds); and trailing-edge flaps to give extra drag to slow down the aeroplane on landing.

HYDRAULIC JACKS, FILLED WITH OIL UNDER HIGH PRESSURE, PROVIDE AN ENORMOUS FORCE FOR MOVING CONTROL SURFACES

The cockpit
Most transport aircraft, such as this Boeing 747, have a cockpit that seats two pilots (*see below, right*). Each pilot has a set of controls. A wheel is turned to roll the aircraft, or is pushed or pulled to make it dive or climb, and there are pedals for the rudder.

THERE ARE FOUR MAIN LANDING GEARS – EACH HAS FOUR WHEELS

THE PILOTS USE A MECHANICAL SYSTEM OF CABLES TO CONTROL THE JACKS AND FLAPS

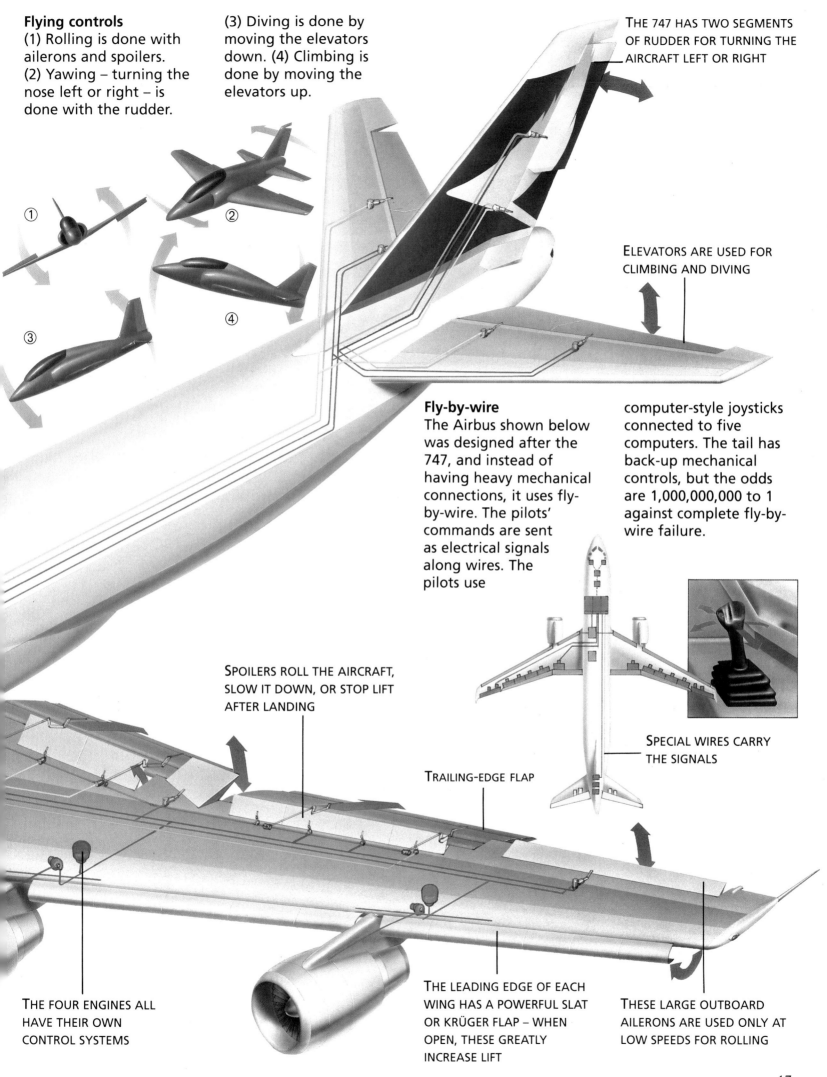

Flying controls
(1) Rolling is done with ailerons and spoilers.
(2) Yawing – turning the nose left or right – is done with the rudder.

(3) Diving is done by moving the elevators down. (4) Climbing is done by moving the elevators up.

THE 747 HAS TWO SEGMENTS OF RUDDER FOR TURNING THE AIRCRAFT LEFT OR RIGHT

ELEVATORS ARE USED FOR CLIMBING AND DIVING

Fly-by-wire
The Airbus shown below was designed after the 747, and instead of having heavy mechanical connections, it uses fly-by-wire. The pilots' commands are sent as electrical signals along wires. The pilots use computer-style joysticks connected to five computers. The tail has back-up mechanical controls, but the odds are 1,000,000,000 to 1 against complete fly-by-wire failure.

SPOILERS ROLL THE AIRCRAFT, SLOW IT DOWN, OR STOP LIFT AFTER LANDING

SPECIAL WIRES CARRY THE SIGNALS

TRAILING-EDGE FLAP

THE FOUR ENGINES ALL HAVE THEIR OWN CONTROL SYSTEMS

THE LEADING EDGE OF EACH WING HAS A POWERFUL SLAT OR KRÜGER FLAP – WHEN OPEN, THESE GREATLY INCREASE LIFT

THESE LARGE OUTBOARD AILERONS ARE USED ONLY AT LOW SPEEDS FOR ROLLING

Control Surfaces

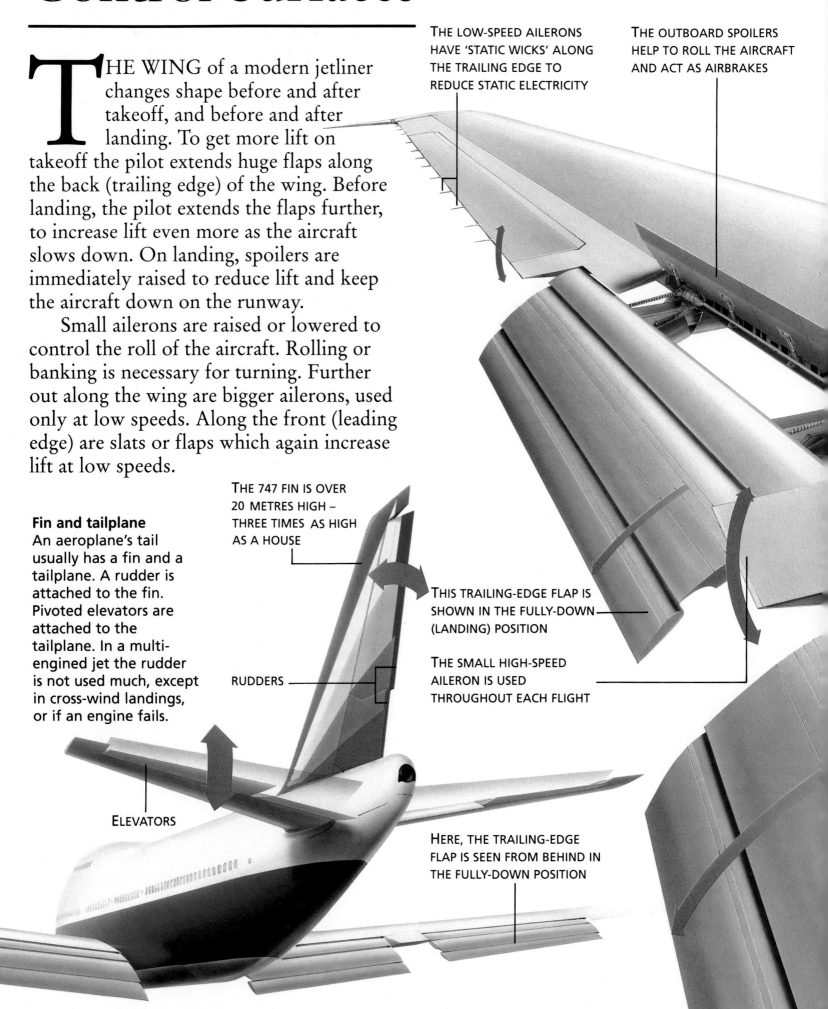

THE WING of a modern jetliner changes shape before and after takeoff, and before and after landing. To get more lift on takeoff the pilot extends huge flaps along the back (trailing edge) of the wing. Before landing, the pilot extends the flaps further, to increase lift even more as the aircraft slows down. On landing, spoilers are immediately raised to reduce lift and keep the aircraft down on the runway.

Small ailerons are raised or lowered to control the roll of the aircraft. Rolling or banking is necessary for turning. Further out along the wing are bigger ailerons, used only at low speeds. Along the front (leading edge) are slats or flaps which again increase lift at low speeds.

Fin and tailplane
An aeroplane's tail usually has a fin and a tailplane. A rudder is attached to the fin. Pivoted elevators are attached to the tailplane. In a multi-engined jet the rudder is not used much, except in cross-wind landings, or if an engine fails.

THE LOW-SPEED AILERONS HAVE 'STATIC WICKS' ALONG THE TRAILING EDGE TO REDUCE STATIC ELECTRICITY

THE OUTBOARD SPOILERS HELP TO ROLL THE AIRCRAFT AND ACT AS AIRBRAKES

THE 747 FIN IS OVER 20 METRES HIGH – THREE TIMES AS HIGH AS A HOUSE

THIS TRAILING-EDGE FLAP IS SHOWN IN THE FULLY-DOWN (LANDING) POSITION

THE SMALL HIGH-SPEED AILERON IS USED THROUGHOUT EACH FLIGHT

RUDDERS

ELEVATORS

HERE, THE TRAILING-EDGE FLAP IS SEEN FROM BEHIND IN THE FULLY-DOWN POSITION

HIDDEN FROM VIEW ARE TEN
SECTIONS OF LEADING-EDGE
FLAP, HINGED DOWN FOR
TAKEOFF OR LANDING

Flaps and spoilers
When a wing changes shape the airflow is affected, and the speed and direction of the aircraft is altered. A trailing-edge flap is lowered to increase drag and slow the aircraft down (*below left*). The leading-edge flaps are extended to give the extra lift needed at a low speed. When spoilers are raised (*below right*), the airflow pushes the wing down, and there is even more drag, and less lift.

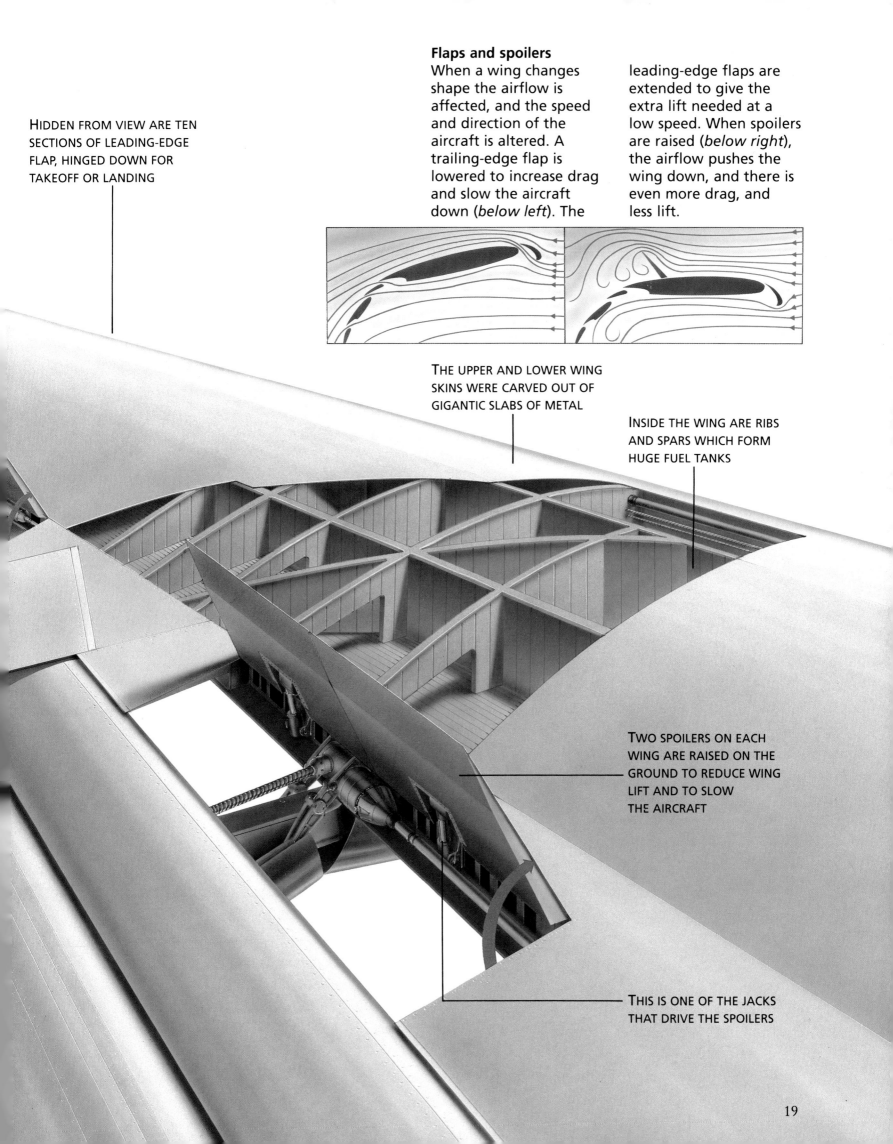

THE UPPER AND LOWER WING
SKINS WERE CARVED OUT OF
GIGANTIC SLABS OF METAL

INSIDE THE WING ARE RIBS
AND SPARS WHICH FORM
HUGE FUEL TANKS

TWO SPOILERS ON EACH
WING ARE RAISED ON THE
GROUND TO REDUCE WING
LIFT AND TO SLOW
THE AIRCRAFT

THIS IS ONE OF THE JACKS
THAT DRIVE THE SPOILERS

Inside the Cockpit

BY 1970 aircraft cockpits had so many instruments and switches, it was difficult to see if everything was all right. Then came the revolutionary new cockpit (*right*). The cockpit in the modern Airbus 340 has only six big colour screens on which the captain (on the left) and the co-pilot (on the right) can see all the information they need. The pilot flies with pedals, and a sidestick held by one hand. Under the side windows are the nosewheel tillers for steering the Airbus on the ground. Overhead are the controls for the fuel, hydraulics, electrical systems, cabin pressurization, and air-conditioning, as well as de-icing, emergency oxygen, and other systems. Below the windscreens are controls for the autopilot. The autopilot keeps the aeroplane on a course which has already been set.

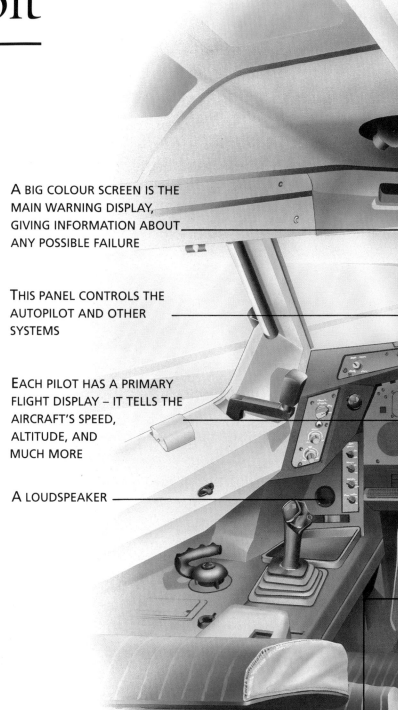

A BIG COLOUR SCREEN IS THE MAIN WARNING DISPLAY, GIVING INFORMATION ABOUT ANY POSSIBLE FAILURE

THIS PANEL CONTROLS THE AUTOPILOT AND OTHER SYSTEMS

EACH PILOT HAS A PRIMARY FLIGHT DISPLAY – IT TELLS THE AIRCRAFT'S SPEED, ALTITUDE, AND MUCH MORE

A LOUDSPEAKER

RUDDER PEDALS ARE USED TO APPLY THE BRAKES AFTER LANDING

Early cockpit
This is a cockpit from about 70 years ago. There are just a few traditional instruments. Two ignition switches (*left of centre*) are switched on before starting the engine. A compass for navigation is set into the bottom of the panel.

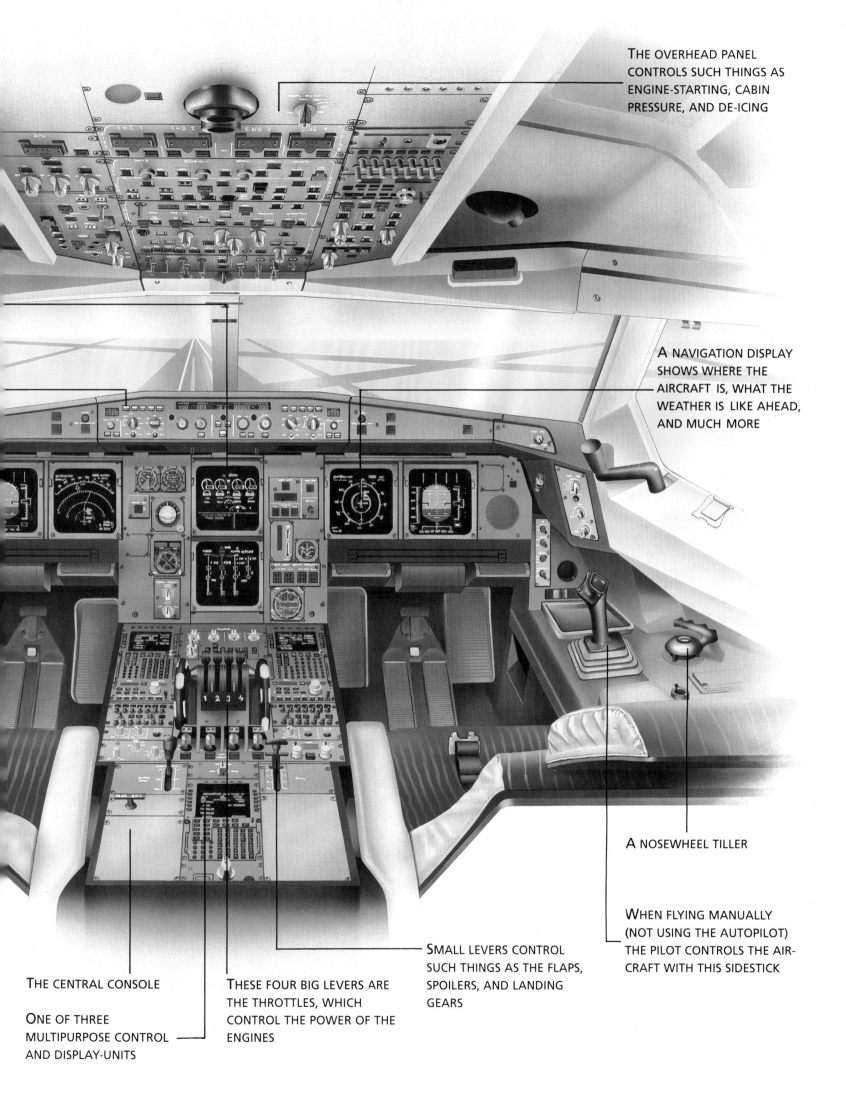

THE OVERHEAD PANEL CONTROLS SUCH THINGS AS ENGINE-STARTING, CABIN PRESSURE, AND DE-ICING

A NAVIGATION DISPLAY SHOWS WHERE THE AIRCRAFT IS, WHAT THE WEATHER IS LIKE AHEAD, AND MUCH MORE

A NOSEWHEEL TILLER

WHEN FLYING MANUALLY (NOT USING THE AUTOPILOT) THE PILOT CONTROLS THE AIRCRAFT WITH THIS SIDESTICK

SMALL LEVERS CONTROL SUCH THINGS AS THE FLAPS, SPOILERS, AND LANDING GEARS

THE CENTRAL CONSOLE

ONE OF THREE MULTIPURPOSE CONTROL AND DISPLAY-UNITS

THESE FOUR BIG LEVERS ARE THE THROTTLES, WHICH CONTROL THE POWER OF THE ENGINES

Parts of an Aeroplane

ONLY A VERY few aeroplanes, such as the US Air Force B-2 'stealth bomber', are just flying wings without a body. Most have a body, called the fuselage, and a tail. The tail usually consists of a fixed vertical fin, to which the rudder is hinged, and fixed tailplanes, to which the elevators are hinged. Modern fighters, such as the F-16 Fighting Falcon (*see right*), have one-piece pivoted tailplanes. These are used instead of elevators for climbing and diving. A great deal of the F-16's fuselage is crammed with electronics, fuel, and the big engine with its air duct. The pilot sits, or almost lies, in a sloping ejection seat at the front. There is a perfect all-round view through the canopy.

The parts for F-16s are made in factories in many countries, but all of them have to fit together perfectly when they get to the final assembly line. Some parts are joined together by rivets, others by screws or bolts. The F-16 is so strong it can out-manoeuvre almost any other aircraft.

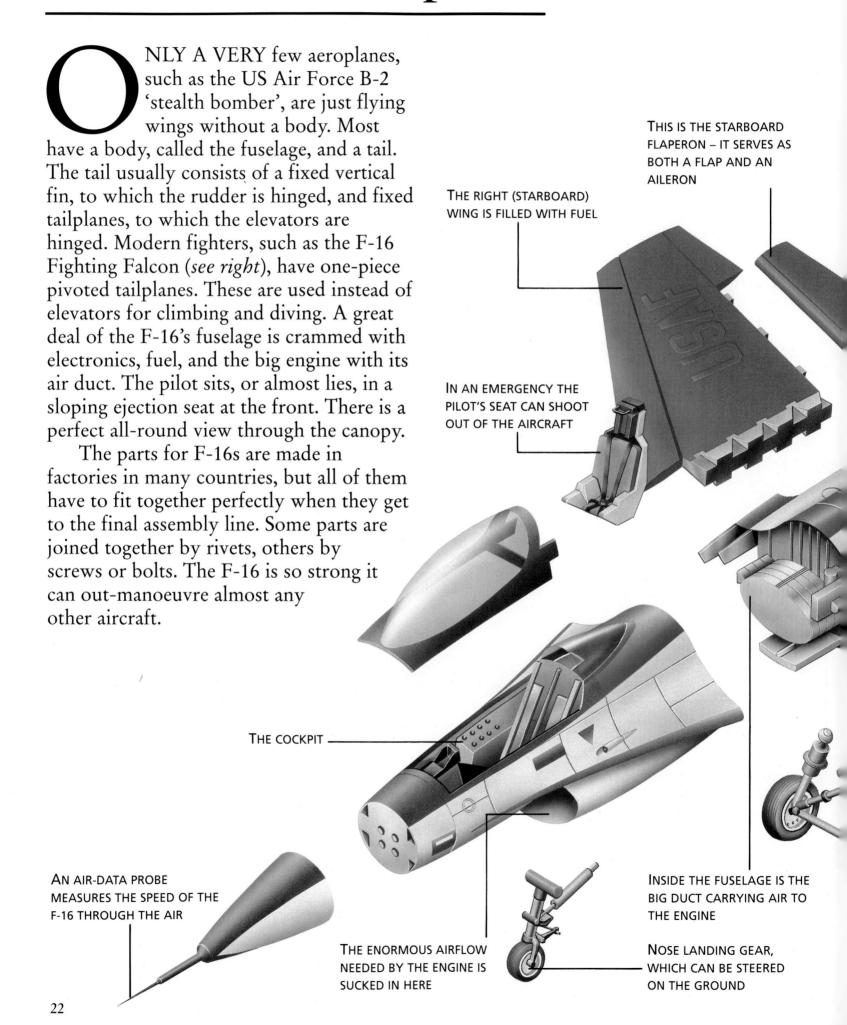

THIS IS THE STARBOARD FLAPERON – IT SERVES AS BOTH A FLAP AND AN AILERON

THE RIGHT (STARBOARD) WING IS FILLED WITH FUEL

IN AN EMERGENCY THE PILOT'S SEAT CAN SHOOT OUT OF THE AIRCRAFT

THE COCKPIT

AN AIR-DATA PROBE MEASURES THE SPEED OF THE F-16 THROUGH THE AIR

THE ENORMOUS AIRFLOW NEEDED BY THE ENGINE IS SUCKED IN HERE

INSIDE THE FUSELAGE IS THE BIG DUCT CARRYING AIR TO THE ENGINE

NOSE landing gear, WHICH CAN BE STEERED ON THE GROUND

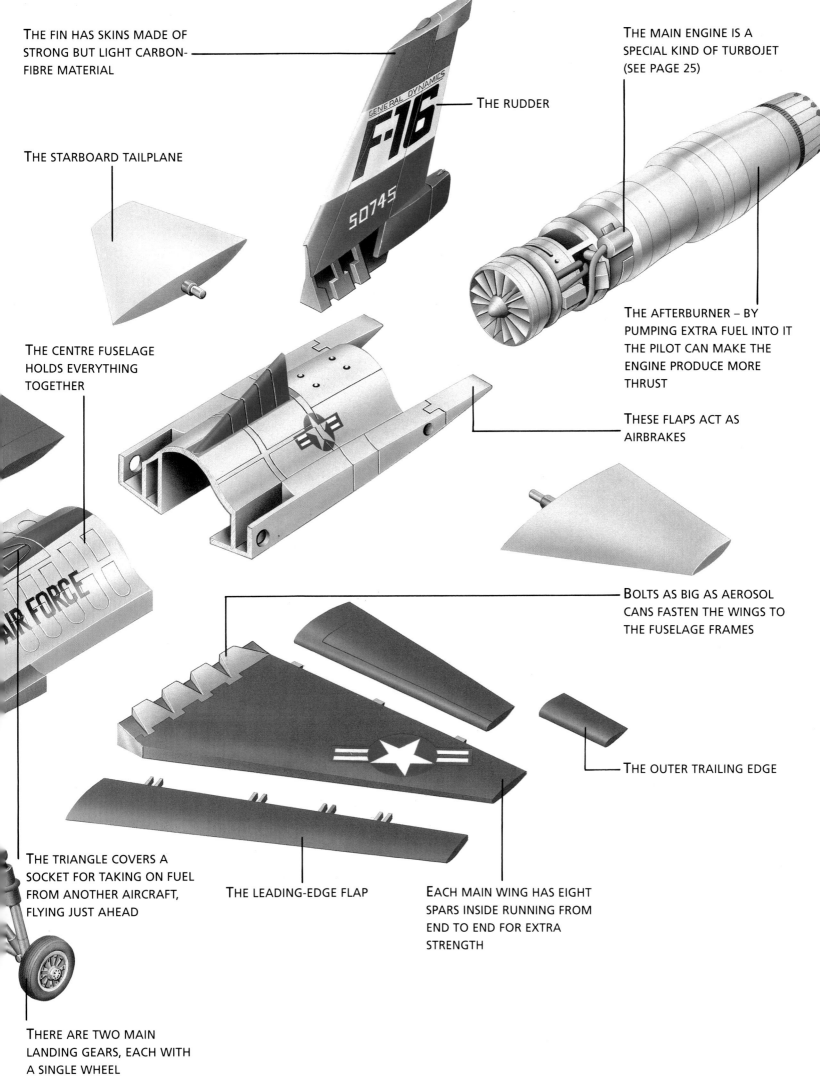

THE FIN HAS SKINS MADE OF STRONG BUT LIGHT CARBON-FIBRE MATERIAL

THE RUDDER

THE STARBOARD TAILPLANE

THE MAIN ENGINE IS A SPECIAL KIND OF TURBOJET (SEE PAGE 25)

F-16

GENERAL DYNAMICS

50745

THE CENTRE FUSELAGE HOLDS EVERYTHING TOGETHER

THE AFTERBURNER – BY PUMPING EXTRA FUEL INTO IT THE PILOT CAN MAKE THE ENGINE PRODUCE MORE THRUST

THESE FLAPS ACT AS AIRBRAKES

AIR FORCE

BOLTS AS BIG AS AEROSOL CANS FASTEN THE WINGS TO THE FUSELAGE FRAMES

THE OUTER TRAILING EDGE

THE TRIANGLE COVERS A SOCKET FOR TAKING ON FUEL FROM ANOTHER AIRCRAFT, FLYING JUST AHEAD

THE LEADING-EDGE FLAP

EACH MAIN WING HAS EIGHT SPARS INSIDE RUNNING FROM END TO END FOR EXTRA STRENGTH

THERE ARE TWO MAIN LANDING GEARS, EACH WITH A SINGLE WHEEL

Engine Power

THE first aircraft to be built, such as the *Flyer* (*see page 10*), used propellers to push them along. A propeller draws air in at the front and throws it backwards. This thrusts the propeller and aircraft forwards. The jet of air thrown back by the propellers does not travel very fast, so propellers cannot move aircraft faster than about 725 kph. Today the fastest aircraft use turbojet or turbofan engines instead of propellers.

Piston engines
Propellers can be driven by a piston engine which is similar to a car engine. A Continental O-240A piston engine is shown below. It was made by Rolls-Royce, weighed 112 kg, and produced 130 horse-power. In the engine four cylinders contain pistons. Fuel and air are burnt to drive the pistons, which push the crankshaft round. The rotating crankshaft turns the propeller.

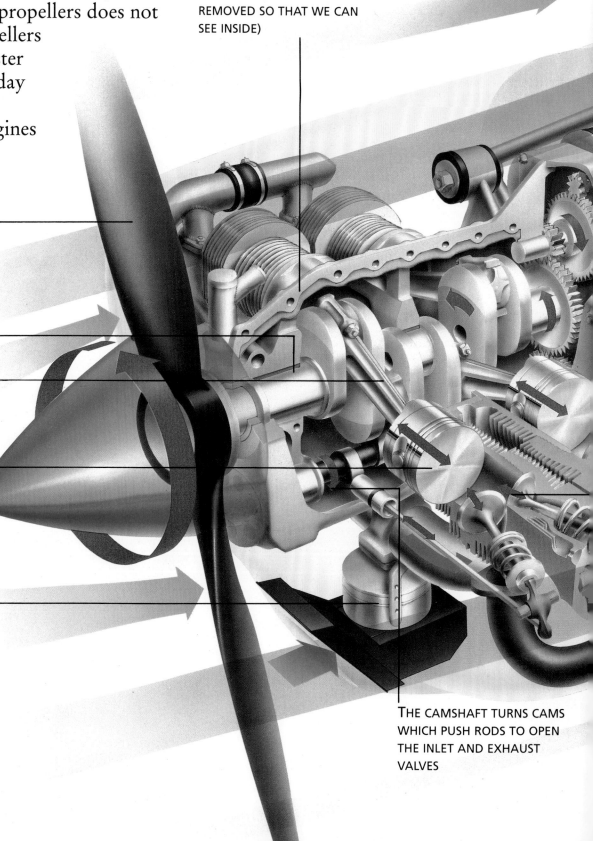

THE CRANKCASE IS A BOX THAT HOLDS THE ENGINE TOGETHER (HALF HAS BEEN REMOVED SO THAT WE CAN SEE INSIDE)

THE THRUST FROM THE PROPELLER PULLS THE AIRCRAFT ALONG

THE CRANKSHAFT ROTATES AND TURNS THE PROPELLERS

RODS JOIN THE PISTONS (WHICH MOVE TO AND FRO) TO THE CRANKSHAFT (WHICH ROTATES)

THE PISTONS INSIDE THE FOUR CYLINDERS ARE DRIVEN BY A RAPIDLY BURNING PETROL AND AIR MIXTURE

THE OIL RADIATOR – IT IS COOLED BY AIR RUSHING THROUGH IT

THE CAMSHAFT TURNS CAMS WHICH PUSH RODS TO OPEN THE INLET AND EXHAUST VALVES

Turboprops

Some propellers are driven by a gas turbine engine, called a turboprop. A turboprop weighing 363 kg can produce about 2,000 horsepower. The main shaft in a turboprop has to be slowed down, using gears like a car's (propellers waste power and make too much noise if they spin too fast). Many airliners carrying 50 to 70 passengers are each powered by two turboprops.

A 'REDUCTION GEAR' HAS TO BE ADDED TO TURN THE PROPELLER ABOUT TEN TIMES MORE SLOWLY

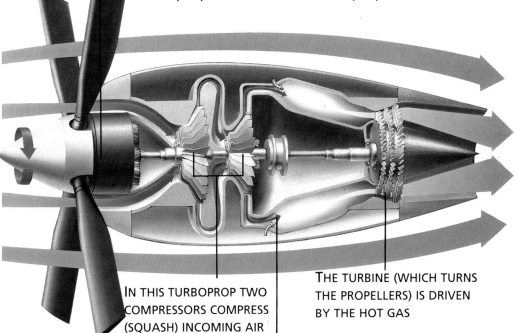

IN THIS TURBOPROP TWO COMPRESSORS COMPRESS (SQUASH) INCOMING AIR

THE TURBINE (WHICH TURNS THE PROPELLERS) IS DRIVEN BY THE HOT GAS

THE FUEL IS SPRAYED IN HERE

THE PETROL AND AIR MIXTURE IS FED THROUGH THIS PIPE

THIS PIPE DISCHARGES THE WHITE-HOT GAS COMING OUT OF THE EXHAUST

Turbojets

Another gas turbine, the turbojet, was first run in 1937. Aircraft driven by turbojet engines do not have propellers. They are propelled by a backward jet of hot gas. These engines, usually in the form of turbofans (*see page 26*), propel all the fastest aircraft.

THE JET OF HOT GAS DRIVES THE AIRCRAFT FORWARDS

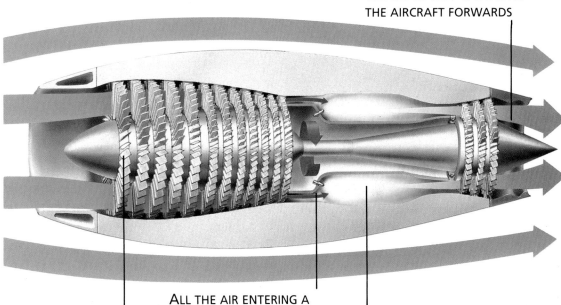

EACH CYLINDER HAS AN INLET VALVE WHICH LETS IN THE PETROL AND AIR MIXTURE

THE COMPRESSORS

ALL THE AIR ENTERING A TURBOJET IS COMPRESSED, AND FORCED INTO THE COMBUSTION CHAMBER

THE COMPRESSED AIR IS HEATED WITH BURNING FUEL

Jet Propulsion

THE jet engine drives an aircraft forward with enormous force. Air is sucked in at the front, compressed by blades, and heated with flames of burning fuel in the combustion chamber. The air is then expelled at a high speed from the back. This stream of hot air – the 'jet' – causes a thrust in the opposite direction (*see below*), propelling the aircraft forwards.

Most big airliners today are powered by turbofan engines, which are quieter and cooler than other jet engines. Air is drawn in by a huge fan spinning at the front. Some of the air passes through the engine, while most flows around the outside, to thrust the aircraft forward. The fan and compressor blades are themselves driven by turbines turned by the stream of hot air rushing out through the back of the engine.

Propulsion

Jet engines work on the principle of jet propulsion. An aircraft is thrust forwards because of a reaction to high-speed air travelling backwards. The same effect can be seen when you release the neck of a blown-up balloon. While the neck is pinched, the air pressure inside is the same in all directions, so the balloon remains still. Because the air is compressed inside, when you release the neck of the balloon the air will rush out at high speed. The air pressure at the opposite end to the neck is no longer counter-balanced, so the balloon flies forwards.

THE ENGINE MOUNTING PYLON

SPINNING FAN BLADES

AIR IS SUCKED IN

A FAN DRIVES SOME OF THE AIR ROUND THE OUTSIDE OF THE ENGINE, TO DRIVE THE AIRCRAFT ALONG

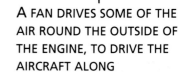

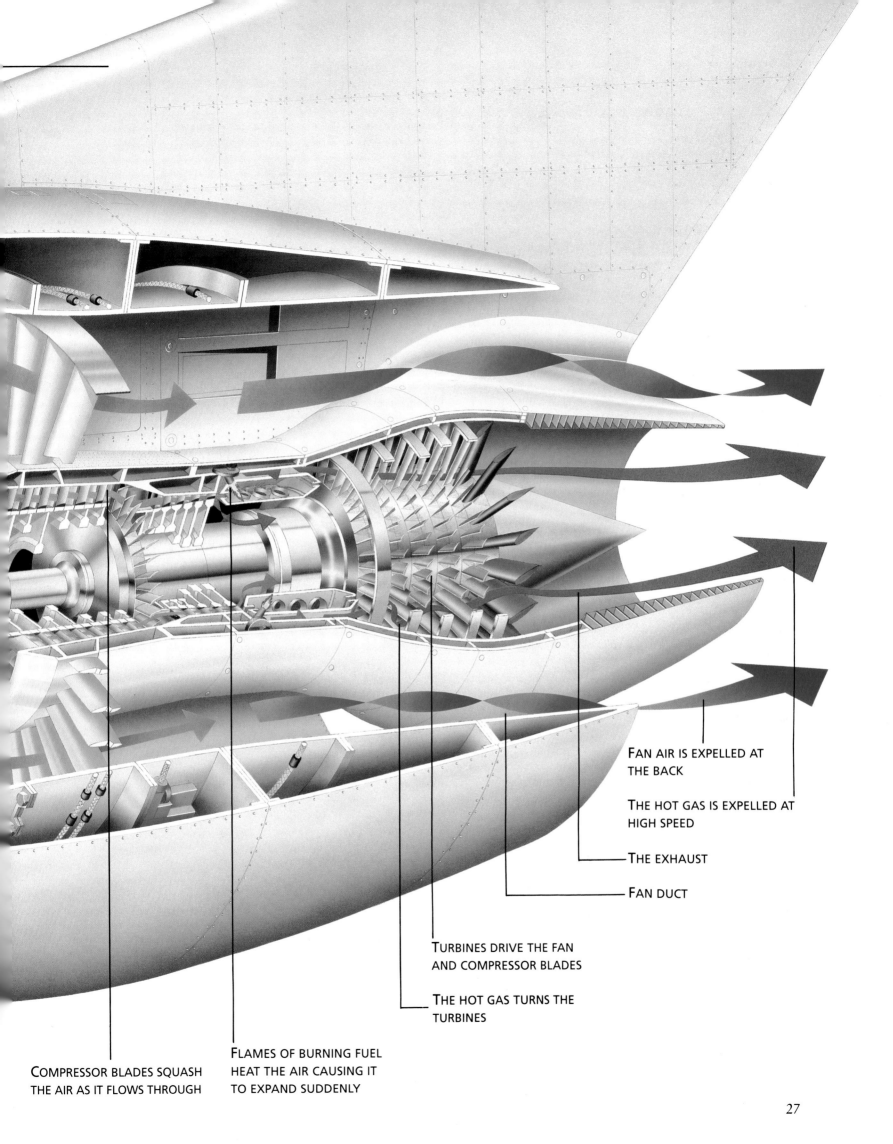

FAN AIR IS EXPELLED AT
THE BACK

THE HOT GAS IS EXPELLED AT
HIGH SPEED

THE EXHAUST

FAN DUCT

TURBINES DRIVE THE FAN
AND COMPRESSOR BLADES

THE HOT GAS TURNS THE
TURBINES

COMPRESSOR BLADES SQUASH
THE AIR AS IT FLOWS THROUGH

FLAMES OF BURNING FUEL
HEAT THE AIR CAUSING IT
TO EXPAND SUDDENLY

Power Systems

LIKE MOST modern aircraft the Boeing 747-400 has powerful electrical and hydraulic systems to help it fly. All its power comes from fuel, carried in enormous tanks. The four engines which burn the fuel drive electric generators, producing nearly 100 horsepower each. Two even more powerful electric generators are driven by the APU (*see top right*). Each engine also drives a hydraulic pump. There are also four pumps driven by high-pressure air. These work four hydraulic systems that pump special liquid to move the landing gear, flaps, flight controls, brakes, and other items. In the belly of the aircraft are the cabin pressurization and air-conditioning systems. When the aircraft is flying high in the sky the air outside is too cold and too thin to breathe, so air for the cabin must be pressurized and kept warm.

AT LEAST 175 TONNES OF FUEL CAN BE PUMPED INTO TANKS IN THE WINGS

TANKS CONTAIN PURE ICED DRINKING WATER FOR THE PASSENGERS

AIRTIGHT PRESSURE BULKHEAD

ELECTRICITY IS NEEDED IN THE GALLEY FOR HEATING THE PASSENGERS' MEALS

AIR ENTERS THE CABIN AIR-CONDITIONING SYSTEM THROUGH INLETS

VERY POWERFUL LAMPS IN THE LEADING-EDGE OF THE WING SWITCH ON BEFORE LANDING

APU

Most modern passenger aircraft have an APU (auxiliary power unit). On the 747 it is at the tip of the tail-end of the fuselage. It is a small gas turbine engine, like a miniature jet engine, driving two electric generators. It also supplies compressed air for starting the main engines and for air-conditioning the cabin. The arrows (*right*) show where air is sucked in and hot exhaust pushed out.

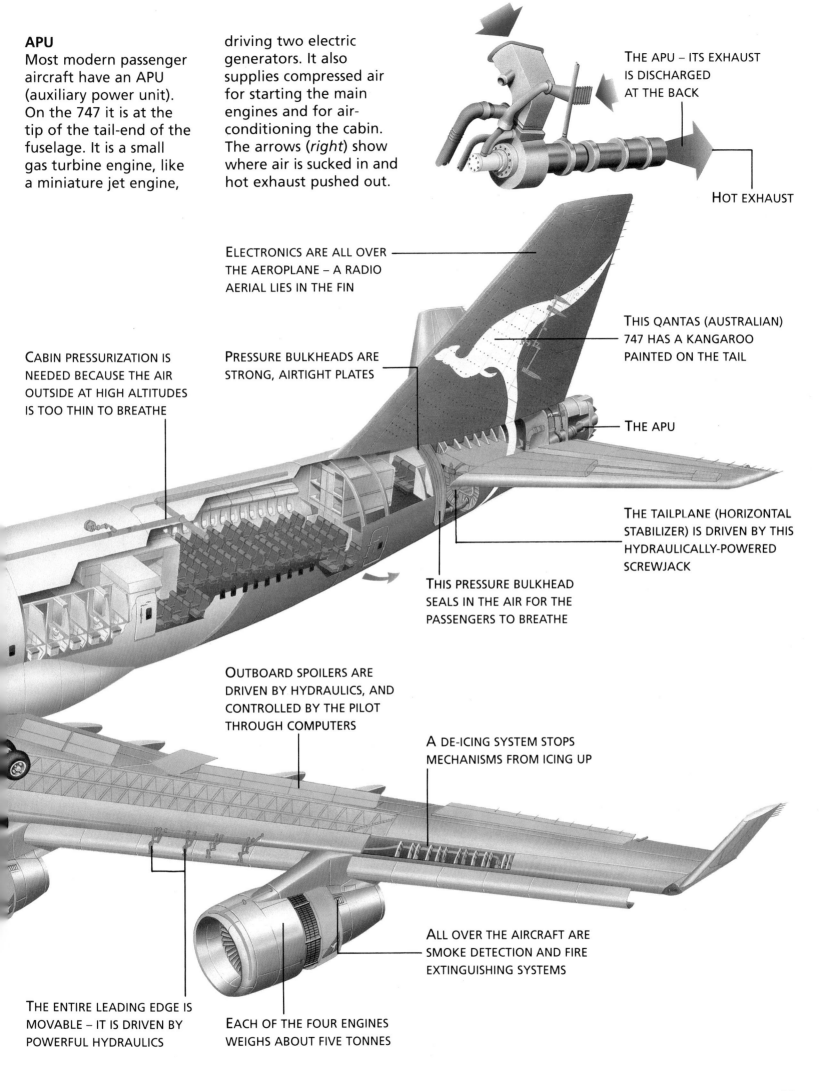

THE APU – ITS EXHAUST IS DISCHARGED AT THE BACK

HOT EXHAUST

ELECTRONICS ARE ALL OVER THE AEROPLANE – A RADIO AERIAL LIES IN THE FIN

THIS QANTAS (AUSTRALIAN) 747 HAS A KANGAROO PAINTED ON THE TAIL

CABIN PRESSURIZATION IS NEEDED BECAUSE THE AIR OUTSIDE AT HIGH ALTITUDES IS TOO THIN TO BREATHE

PRESSURE BULKHEADS ARE STRONG, AIRTIGHT PLATES

THE APU

THE TAILPLANE (HORIZONTAL STABILIZER) IS DRIVEN BY THIS HYDRAULICALLY-POWERED SCREWJACK

THIS PRESSURE BULKHEAD SEALS IN THE AIR FOR THE PASSENGERS TO BREATHE

OUTBOARD SPOILERS ARE DRIVEN BY HYDRAULICS, AND CONTROLLED BY THE PILOT THROUGH COMPUTERS

A DE-ICING SYSTEM STOPS MECHANISMS FROM ICING UP

THE ENTIRE LEADING EDGE IS MOVABLE – IT IS DRIVEN BY POWERFUL HYDRAULICS

EACH OF THE FOUR ENGINES WEIGHS ABOUT FIVE TONNES

ALL OVER THE AIRCRAFT ARE SMOKE DETECTION AND FIRE EXTINGUISHING SYSTEMS

Air-Traffic Control

LIKE CARS on a road, aircraft have to be controlled and obey rules in order to avoid collisions. Big and powerful aircraft keep to invisible 'roads' called airways. Controllers on the ground can watch the progress of each aircraft on radar screens. They can tell which aircraft is which, how high it is, and where it is going. Each aircraft has its own navigation systems to guide it, and stations on the ground called VORs act like airway signposts. When an aircraft reaches its destination, it may have to join a stack (a queue) to await its turn to be guided down to the runway.

ILS

The ILS (instrument landing system) helps aircraft equipped with an ILS receiver to land safely, even in low cloud and fog. It consists of two radio beams, sent from near the runway towards approaching aircraft. One guides the aircraft in direction (left or right). The other guides it vertically (up or down) along the correct glide path.

AIRWAY

AIRPORT

RUNWAY

THE CENTRELINE OF AN ILS RUNWAY – EACH APPROACHING AIRCRAFT IS GUIDED TO IT

THE INNER MARKER

THE OUTER MARKER – THE PILOT KNOWS EXACTLY HOW HIGH THE AIRCRAFT SHOULD BE AS IT PASSES OVER THIS POINT

AN AIRCRAFT HAS 'CAPTURED' THE TWO ILS BEAMS AND IS BEING GUIDED DOWNWARDS

THE LOCALIZER BEAM IS A THIN VERTICAL SHEET GIVING STEERING GUIDANCE (LEFT OR RIGHT)

THE GLIDE SLOPE BEAM IS A THIN HORIZONTAL SHEET GUIDING THE PLANE VERTICALLY (UP OR DOWN)

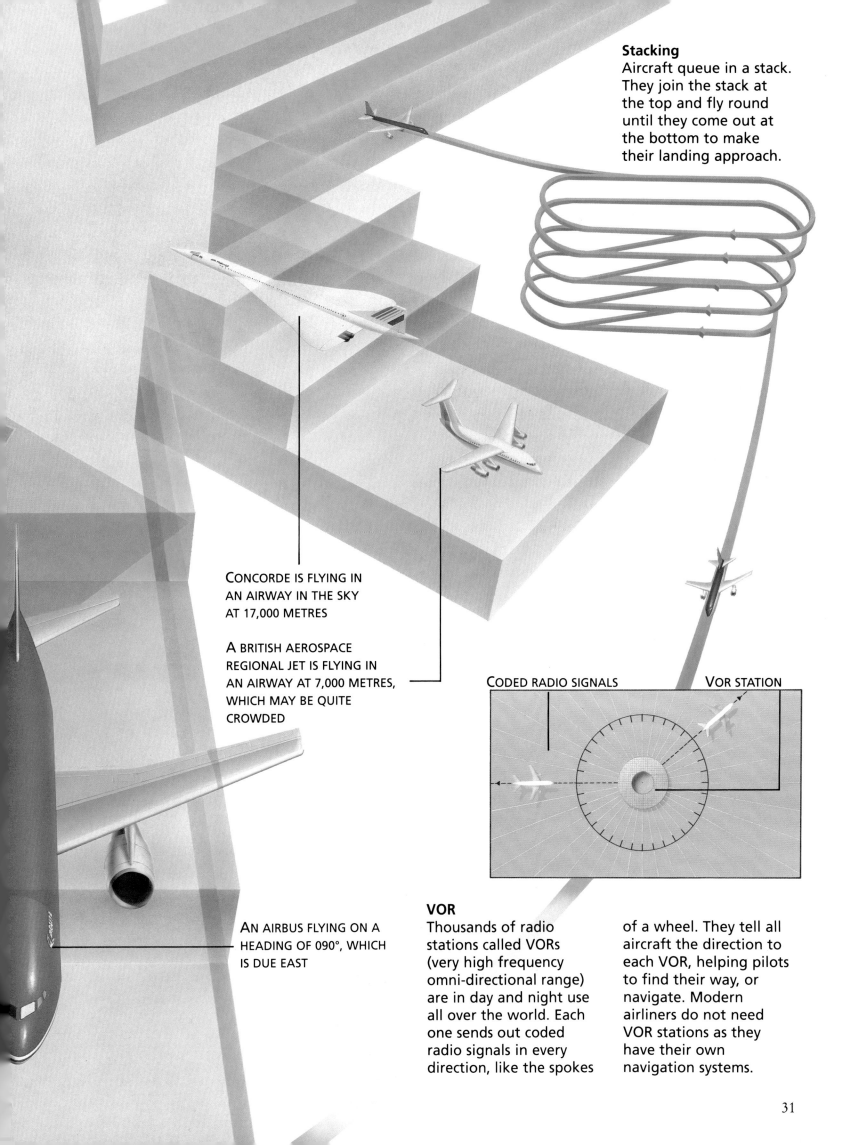

Stacking
Aircraft queue in a stack. They join the stack at the top and fly round until they come out at the bottom to make their landing approach.

CONCORDE IS FLYING IN AN AIRWAY IN THE SKY AT 17,000 METRES

A BRITISH AEROSPACE REGIONAL JET IS FLYING IN AN AIRWAY AT 7,000 METRES, WHICH MAY BE QUITE CROWDED

CODED RADIO SIGNALS   VOR STATION

AN AIRBUS FLYING ON A HEADING OF 090°, WHICH IS DUE EAST

VOR
Thousands of radio stations called VORs (very high frequency omni-directional range) are in day and night use all over the world. Each one sends out coded radio signals in every direction, like the spokes of a wheel. They tell all aircraft the direction to each VOR, helping pilots to find their way, or navigate. Modern airliners do not need VOR stations as they have their own navigation systems.

31

Radar

RADAR is a way of using special radio beams to detect other objects at a great distance, even at night or through clouds. Huge radar stations on the ground can watch the progress of every aircraft in the sky for over 160 kilometres in all directions. Most big or powerful aircraft carry their own radar. The main one will be in the nose, looking ahead like a car headlamp. In a passenger jet the radar searches for mountains, for other aircraft at the same height (to avoid them), and especially for thunderstorms and clouds which could toss the aircraft about and make passengers feel sick. The captain can steer round turbulence (stormy air) even at night. Fighters and bombers often have a radar at the back to warn if an enemy fighter is trying to catch them from behind. There are even special radars which, fitted into an aircraft flying at a great height, can produce a detailed picture of the ground below.

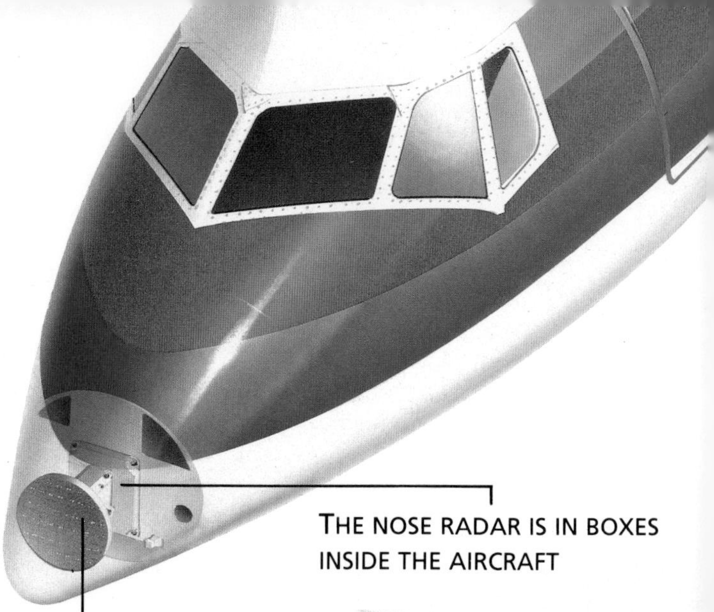

THE NOSE RADAR IS IN BOXES INSIDE THE AIRCRAFT

RADAR BEAMS ARE SENT OUT AND RECEIVED BACK BY THIS ANTENNA

Radar location
The most common place for an aircraft's radar is in its nose. Here, it can be pointed ahead. In a passenger aircraft, such as the BAe Regional Jet seen here, it can show the pilot if there is bad weather ahead.

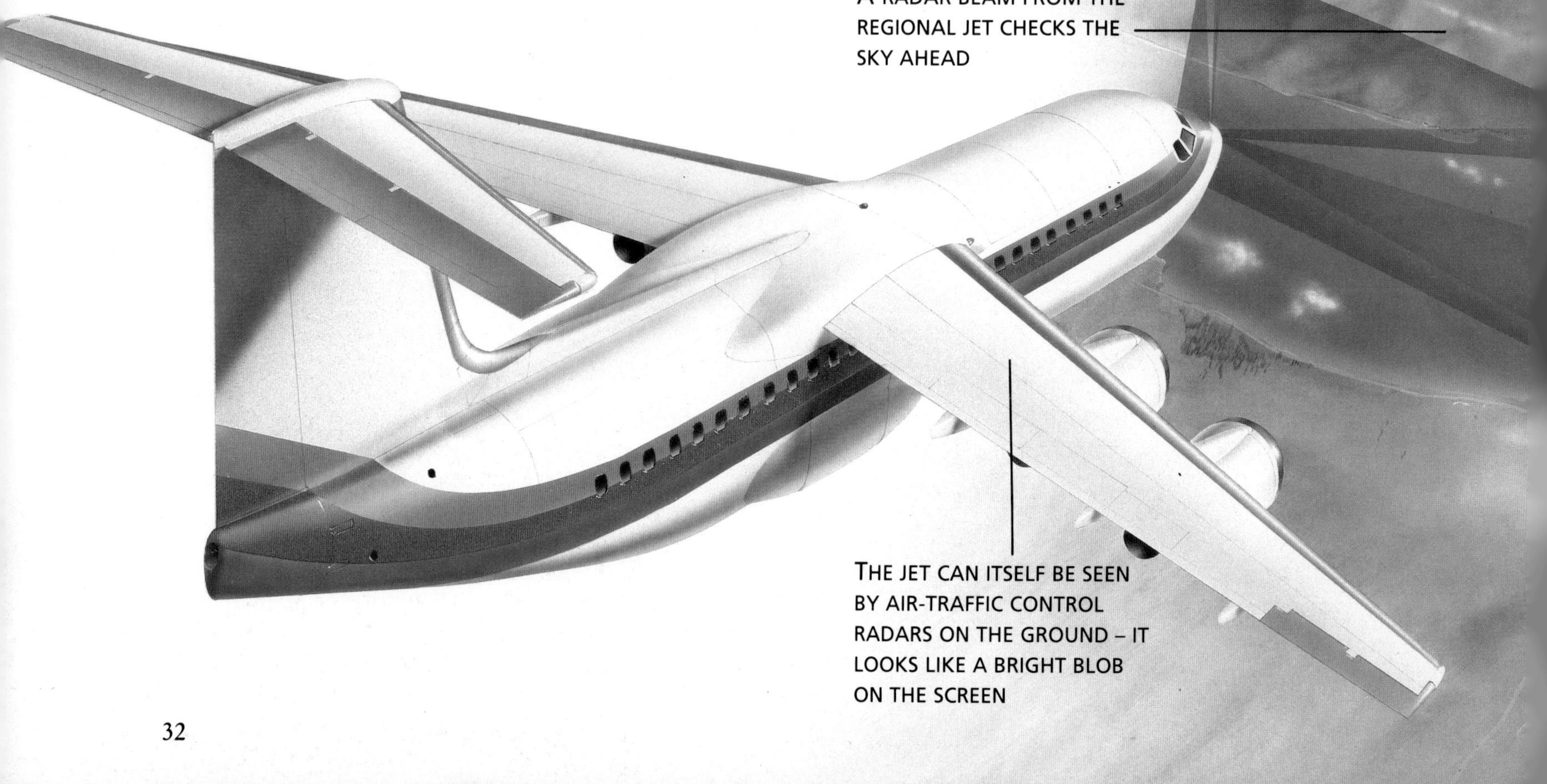

A RADAR BEAM FROM THE REGIONAL JET CHECKS THE SKY AHEAD

THE JET CAN ITSELF BE SEEN BY AIR-TRAFFIC CONTROL RADARS ON THE GROUND – IT LOOKS LIKE A BRIGHT BLOB ON THE SCREEN

Radar altimeter

Ordinary altimeters measure air density, which decreases with height. These cannot tell if an aircraft at 300 metres altitude is heading towards a 600-metre-high mountain. A radar altimeter measures the exact distance to the ground, and would detect the rising land-level of the mountain.

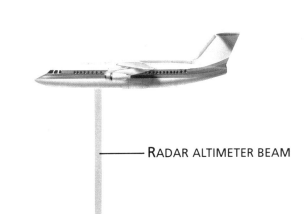

RADAR ALTIMETER BEAM

RADAR ALTIMETER

WITHOUT RADAR, THE PILOT COULD NOT TELL IF THERE WAS VIOLENT TURBULENCE INSIDE A CLOUD, EVEN IN DAYLIGHT

Radar pictures

The picture (*below left*) shows how a radar can warn the pilot of severe turbulence inside clouds (here it is shown in red). The other (*right*) shows ground features, such as hills and coastlines.

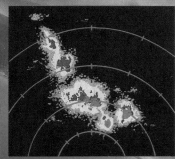

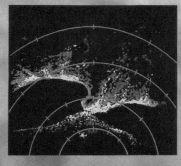

Supersonic Aircraft

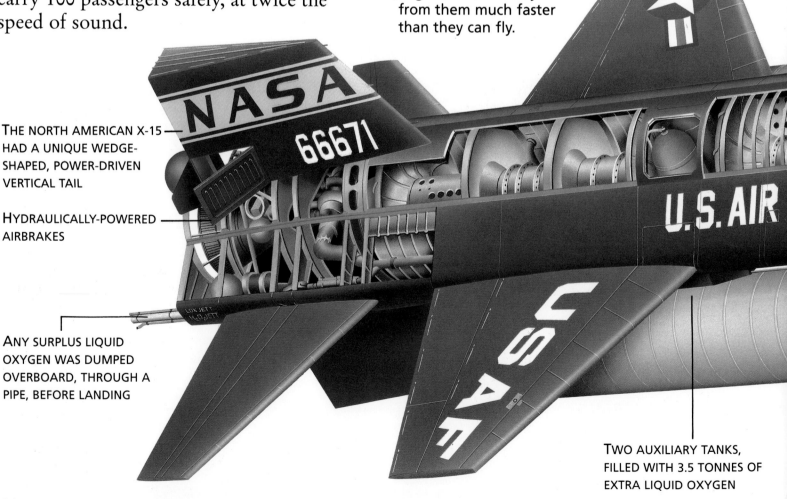

SOUND travels through the air at a speed of about 1,225 kph. If you saw a firework explode three kilometres away, you would not hear the bang for about ten seconds. In 1947 an American, 'Chuck' Yeager, piloted the first aeroplane able to fly faster than sound. Aircraft able to do this are called supersonic. In 1959 an X-15 aeroplane (*see below*) made its first flight. Driven by a rocket, and with only one man aboard, it shot towards space and reached a speed of 7,297 kph, or nearly seven times the speed of sound. This is the fastest any aircraft has flown. In 1969 the first Concorde was finished – the world's first SST (supersonic transport). In many ways this was an even greater achievement than the X-15, because Concordes take off without rockets and can carry 100 passengers safely, at twice the speed of sound.

Subsonic flight
The diagram above shows a Concorde supersonic airliner flying at subsonic speed (much slower than sound). The sound waves spread away like ripples on a pond, those in front of the nose travelling away from it. This happens with all subsonic aircraft. The noise of their engines rushes away from them much faster than they can fly.

THESE SOUND WAVES ARE FROM THE NOISE OF THE AIRCRAFT'S ENGINES

IN AIRLESS SPACE THE PILOT CONTROLLED THE X-15 WITH SMALL REACTION JETS, LIKE TINY ROCKETS

THE NORTH AMERICAN X-15 HAD A UNIQUE WEDGE-SHAPED, POWER-DRIVEN VERTICAL TAIL

HYDRAULICALLY-POWERED AIRBRAKES

ANY SURPLUS LIQUID OXYGEN WAS DUMPED OVERBOARD, THROUGH A PIPE, BEFORE LANDING

TWO AUXILIARY TANKS, FILLED WITH 3.5 TONNES OF EXTRA LIQUID OXYGEN

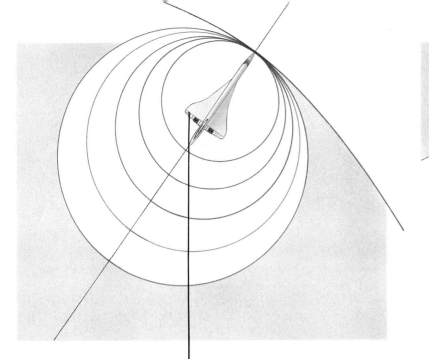

SUPERSONIC AIRCRAFT OFTEN HAVE A POINTED NOSE AND TAPERED WINGS

At the speed of sound
The diagram above shows a Concorde flying at Mach 1, which is exactly the same speed as sound. All the aircraft's sound waves bunch together at the nose. The aircraft is moving forward at the same speed as the waves themselves.

Mach 2
Concorde normally flies at Mach 2 (twice as fast as sound). The aircraft's sound waves travel away at the same speed as before, but Concorde punches ahead much faster. Concorde is specially shaped so that its wings stay within the sound waves and the pilot can keep control of the aircraft.

SOUND FROM A SUPERSONIC AIRCRAFT FORMS A CONE

AMMONIA, KEPT HERE, WAS MIXED WITH THE LIQUID OXYGEN TO DRIVE THE ROCKET ENGINE

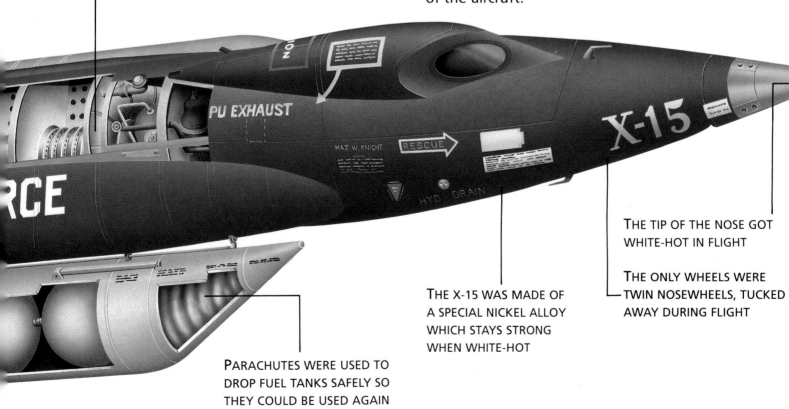

THE TIP OF THE NOSE GOT WHITE-HOT IN FLIGHT

THE ONLY WHEELS WERE TWIN NOSEWHEELS, TUCKED AWAY DURING FLIGHT

THE X-15 WAS MADE OF A SPECIAL NICKEL ALLOY WHICH STAYS STRONG WHEN WHITE-HOT

PARACHUTES WERE USED TO DROP FUEL TANKS SAFELY SO THEY COULD BE USED AGAIN

VTOL Aircraft

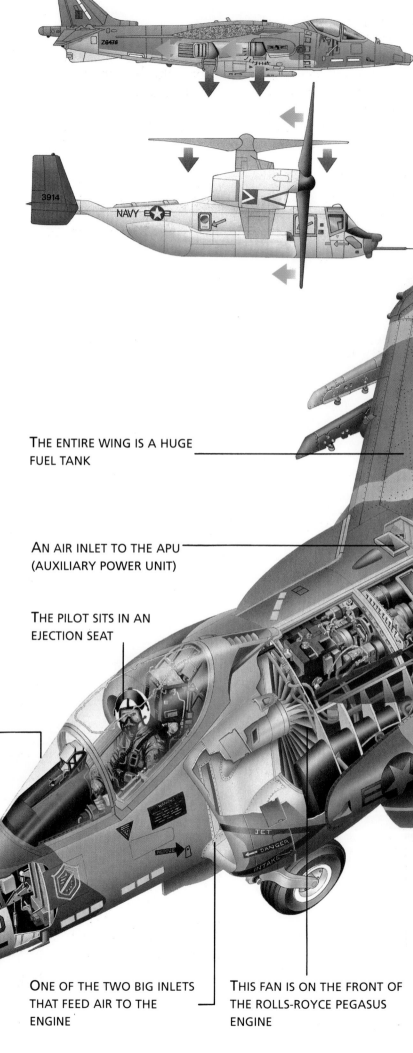

VTOL STANDS for Vertical Take-Off and Landing. To get off the ground, ordinary aeroplanes have to reach a high speed while travelling down a long runway, before their wings generate a lift greater than the aircraft's weight. Before 1960, only helicopters could go straight up and land on a small area like a back garden, and they were slow. However, in 1960 a British team of engineers produced a little aeroplane with a special jet engine with two nozzles on each side. These jet nozzles could be rotated to point downwards to lift the aircraft into the sky. Then they could be rotated to point backwards to push the aircraft along at high speed. This led to the unique Harrier warplane (*right*), the only fixed-wing combat aircraft that cannot be destroyed on the ground because it can hide in forests or even cities.

THE ENTIRE WING IS A HUGE FUEL TANK

AN AIR INLET TO THE APU (AUXILIARY POWER UNIT)

THE PILOT SITS IN AN EJECTION SEAT

THE WINDSCREEN HAS TO BE STRONG ENOUGH TO WITHSTAND HITTING ITEMS, LIKE BIRDS, AT 800 KPH

THE NOSE OF THE HARRIER IS FILLED WITH AVIONICS (AVIATION ELECTRONICS)

ONE OF THE TWO BIG INLETS THAT FEED AIR TO THE ENGINE

THIS FAN IS ON THE FRONT OF THE ROLLS-ROYCE PEGASUS ENGINE

Harrier and V-22 Osprey

The Harrier (*top left*) has a special turbofan engine with four nozzles, two on each side. These can swivel and point down to lift the Harrier. When they point backwards they can drive it at the speed of sound. The V-22 Osprey (*bottom left*) can also land and take-off vertically. It has two big prop-rotors. When they are tilted up they act like rotors and lift the Osprey. When tilted forwards they act like propellers and pull it at 560 kph. The Osprey can do everything a helicopter can do, but it can fly twice as fast and more than twice as far.

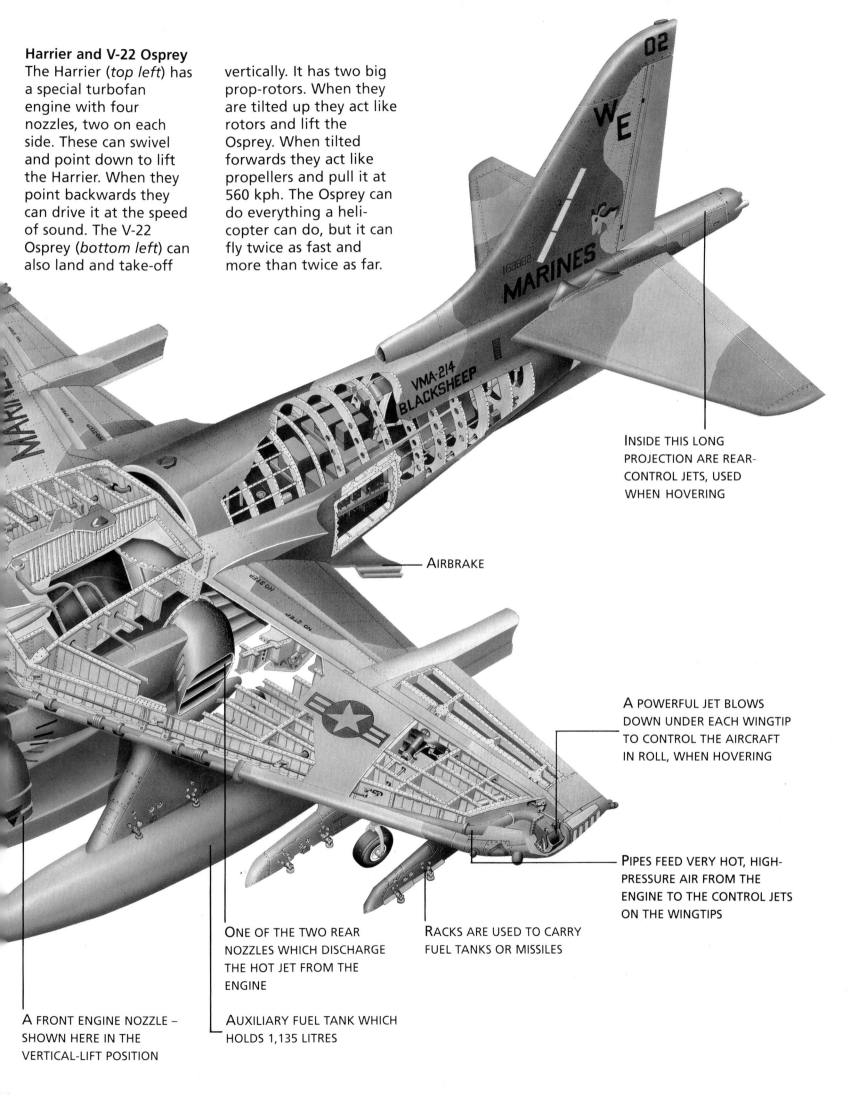

INSIDE THIS LONG PROJECTION ARE REAR-CONTROL JETS, USED WHEN HOVERING

AIRBRAKE

A POWERFUL JET BLOWS DOWN UNDER EACH WINGTIP TO CONTROL THE AIRCRAFT IN ROLL, WHEN HOVERING

PIPES FEED VERY HOT, HIGH-PRESSURE AIR FROM THE ENGINE TO THE CONTROL JETS ON THE WINGTIPS

ONE OF THE TWO REAR NOZZLES WHICH DISCHARGE THE HOT JET FROM THE ENGINE

RACKS ARE USED TO CARRY FUEL TANKS OR MISSILES

A FRONT ENGINE NOZZLE – SHOWN HERE IN THE VERTICAL-LIFT POSITION

AUXILIARY FUEL TANK WHICH HOLDS 1,135 LITRES

Microlights

FROM 1920 people had tried to design tiny aeroplanes that would be as popular as cars. Around 1960 a new kind of wing called the Rogallo was introduced which led to the popular sport of hang-gliding. It was shaped like a triangle, flying point first. A light framework of metal tubing was added underneath to support a person. Soon thousands of people were hang-gliding. Such gliders in turn led to little aeroplanes, with the pilot seated on or inside a tiny craft with a pusher engine at the back. Some of these 'microlights' have Rogallo wings, but today most have simple rigid wings like the one shown here. The modern 'micro' consists of a wing and a 'trike unit' (so called because it is a tricycle). A few are autogyros, which have a rotor instead of a wing. The rotor is spun round by the air flowing past. All these micros can fly at about 100 kph.

Autogyros

The autogyro above is a Wallis WA 116, used for displays and filming. The pilot sits in a streamlined casing, with an open cockpit. A helmet and goggles are necessary because the pusher propeller can drive the WA 116 at 160 kph. The air rushing past the two-blade rotor keeps it rotating, so that the blades provide lift. Wing

Commander Wallis has made his little autogyros so stable the pilot can safely take his or her hands and feet off the controls.

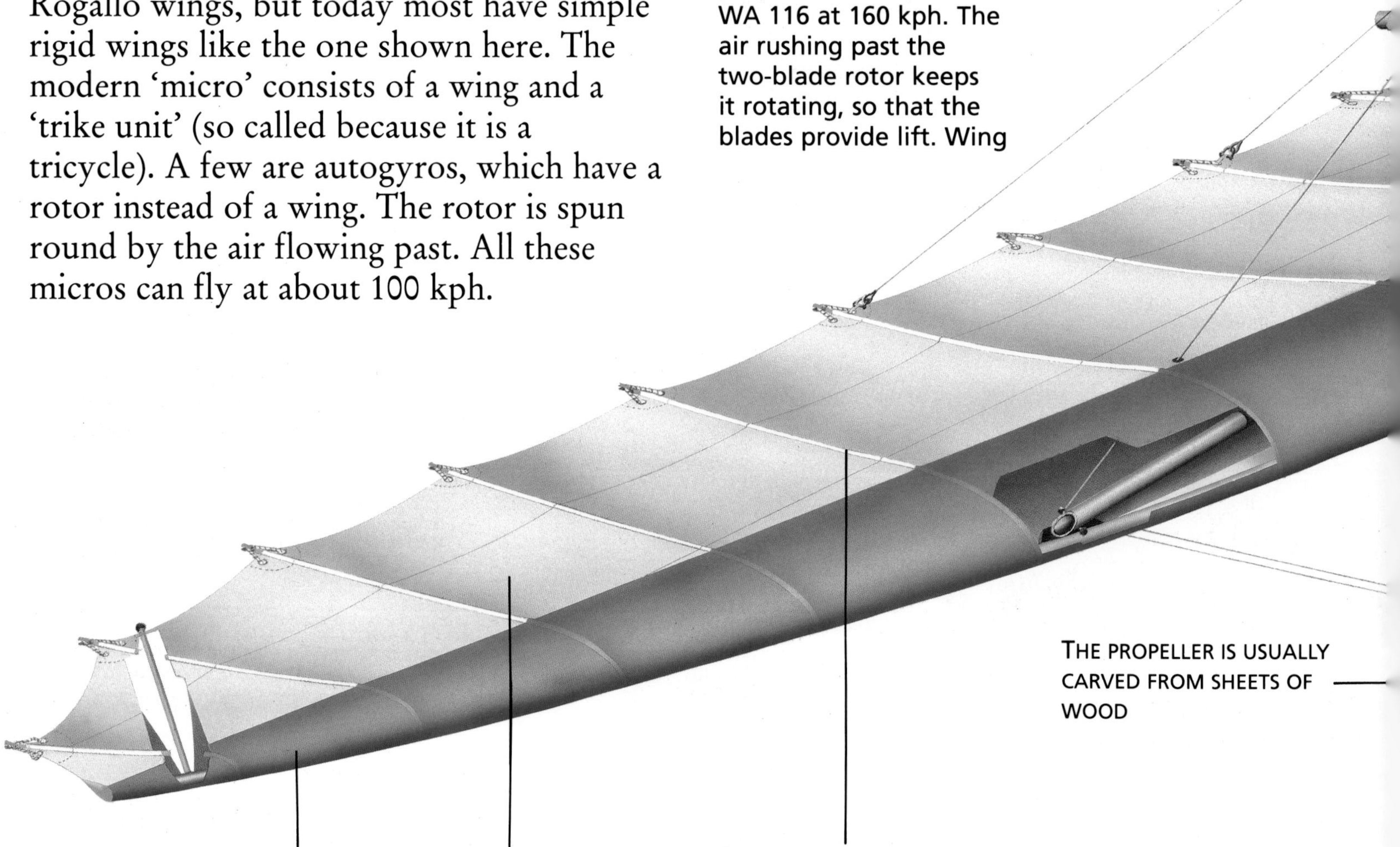

THE PROPELLER IS USUALLY CARVED FROM SHEETS OF WOOD

ALUMINIUM RODS KEEP THE WINGS IN PLACE

TO KEEP ITS SHAPE THE LEADING EDGE IS USUALLY STIFFENED WITH A SHEET OF PLASTIC

THE WING MUST BE BROAD TO LIFT ITS HEAVY LOAD

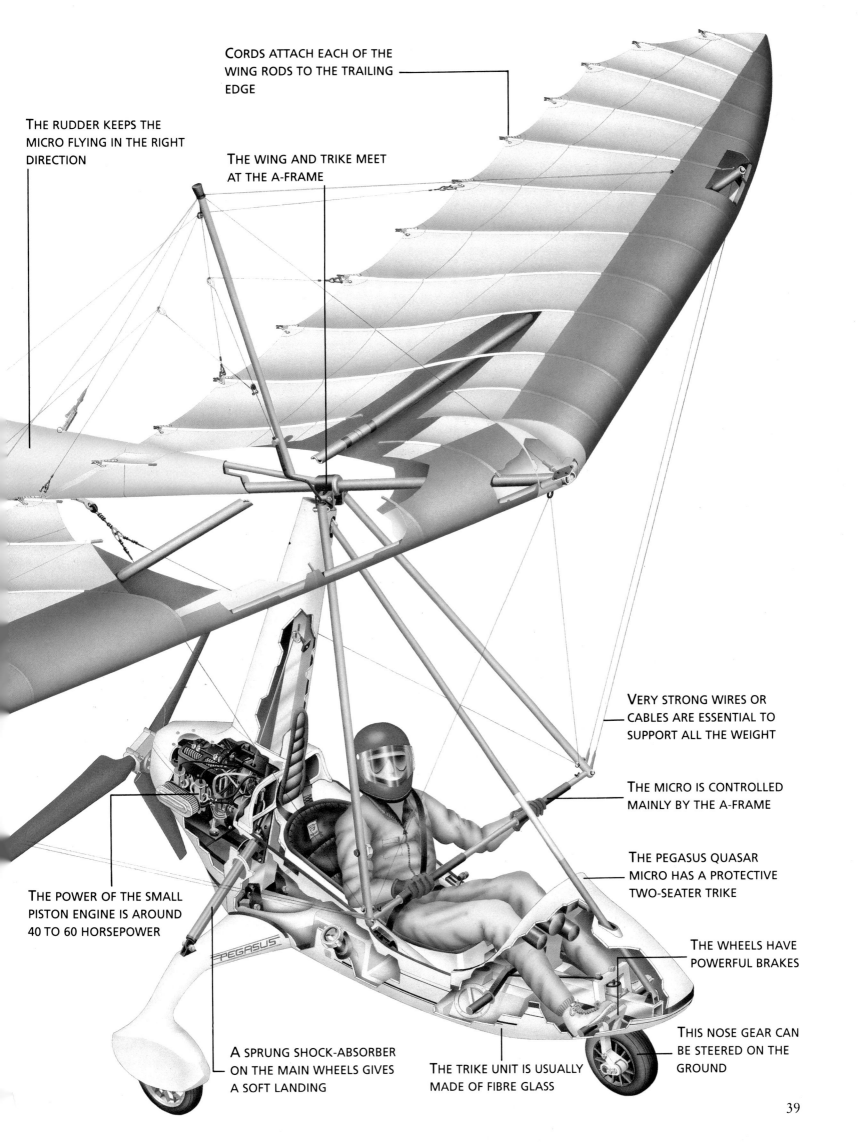

CORDS ATTACH EACH OF THE WING RODS TO THE TRAILING EDGE

THE RUDDER KEEPS THE MICRO FLYING IN THE RIGHT DIRECTION

THE WING AND TRIKE MEET AT THE A-FRAME

VERY STRONG WIRES OR CABLES ARE ESSENTIAL TO SUPPORT ALL THE WEIGHT

THE MICRO IS CONTROLLED MAINLY BY THE A-FRAME

THE PEGASUS QUASAR MICRO HAS A PROTECTIVE TWO-SEATER TRIKE

THE POWER OF THE SMALL PISTON ENGINE IS AROUND 40 TO 60 HORSEPOWER

THE WHEELS HAVE POWERFUL BRAKES

A SPRUNG SHOCK-ABSORBER ON THE MAIN WHEELS GIVES A SOFT LANDING

THE TRIKE UNIT IS USUALLY MADE OF FIBRE GLASS

THIS NOSE GEAR CAN BE STEERED ON THE GROUND

39

Human-Powered Aircraft

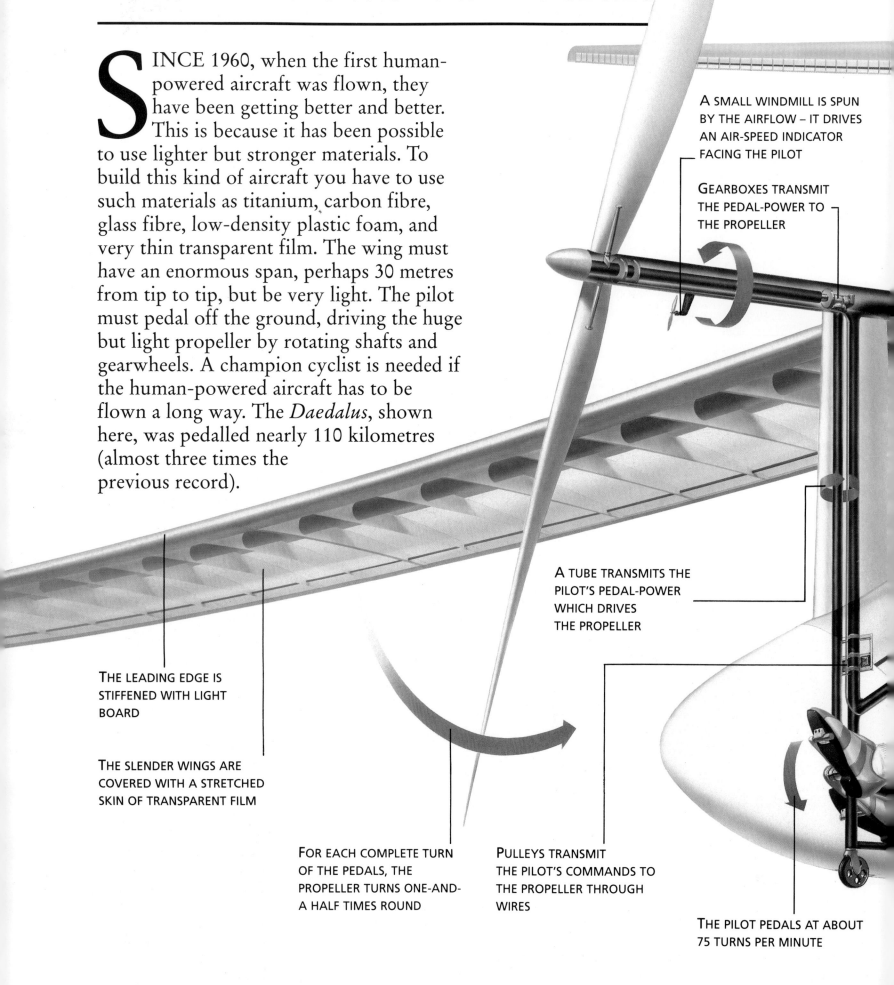

S INCE 1960, when the first human-powered aircraft was flown, they have been getting better and better. This is because it has been possible to use lighter but stronger materials. To build this kind of aircraft you have to use such materials as titanium, carbon fibre, glass fibre, low-density plastic foam, and very thin transparent film. The wing must have an enormous span, perhaps 30 metres from tip to tip, but be very light. The pilot must pedal off the ground, driving the huge but light propeller by rotating shafts and gearwheels. A champion cyclist is needed if the human-powered aircraft has to be flown a long way. The *Daedalus*, shown here, was pedalled nearly 110 kilometres (almost three times the previous record).

A SMALL WINDMILL IS SPUN BY THE AIRFLOW – IT DRIVES AN AIR-SPEED INDICATOR FACING THE PILOT

GEARBOXES TRANSMIT THE PEDAL-POWER TO THE PROPELLER

A TUBE TRANSMITS THE PILOT'S PEDAL-POWER WHICH DRIVES THE PROPELLER

THE LEADING EDGE IS STIFFENED WITH LIGHT BOARD

THE SLENDER WINGS ARE COVERED WITH A STRETCHED SKIN OF TRANSPARENT FILM

FOR EACH COMPLETE TURN OF THE PEDALS, THE PROPELLER TURNS ONE-AND-A HALF TIMES ROUND

PULLEYS TRANSMIT THE PILOT'S COMMANDS TO THE PROPELLER THROUGH WIRES

THE PILOT PEDALS AT ABOUT 75 TURNS PER MINUTE

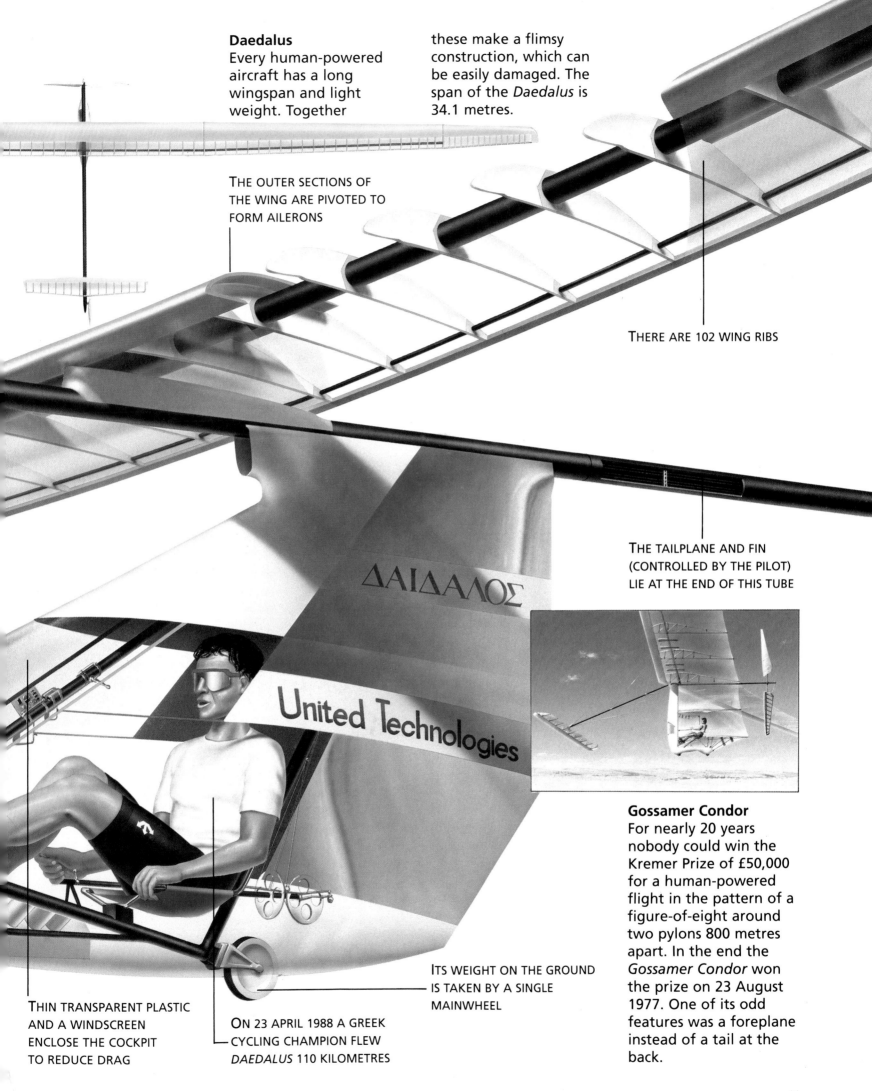

Daedalus
Every human-powered aircraft has a long wingspan and light weight. Together these make a flimsy construction, which can be easily damaged. The span of the *Daedalus* is 34.1 metres.

THE OUTER SECTIONS OF THE WING ARE PIVOTED TO FORM AILERONS

THERE ARE 102 WING RIBS

ΔΑΙΔΑΛΟΣ

United Technologies

THE TAILPLANE AND FIN (CONTROLLED BY THE PILOT) LIE AT THE END OF THIS TUBE

Gossamer Condor
For nearly 20 years nobody could win the Kremer Prize of £50,000 for a human-powered flight in the pattern of a figure-of-eight around two pylons 800 metres apart. In the end the *Gossamer Condor* won the prize on 23 August 1977. One of its odd features was a foreplane instead of a tail at the back.

ITS WEIGHT ON THE GROUND IS TAKEN BY A SINGLE MAINWHEEL

THIN TRANSPARENT PLASTIC AND A WINDSCREEN ENCLOSE THE COCKPIT TO REDUCE DRAG

ON 23 APRIL 1988 A GREEK CYCLING CHAMPION FLEW *DAEDALUS* 110 KILOMETRES

Helicopter Flight

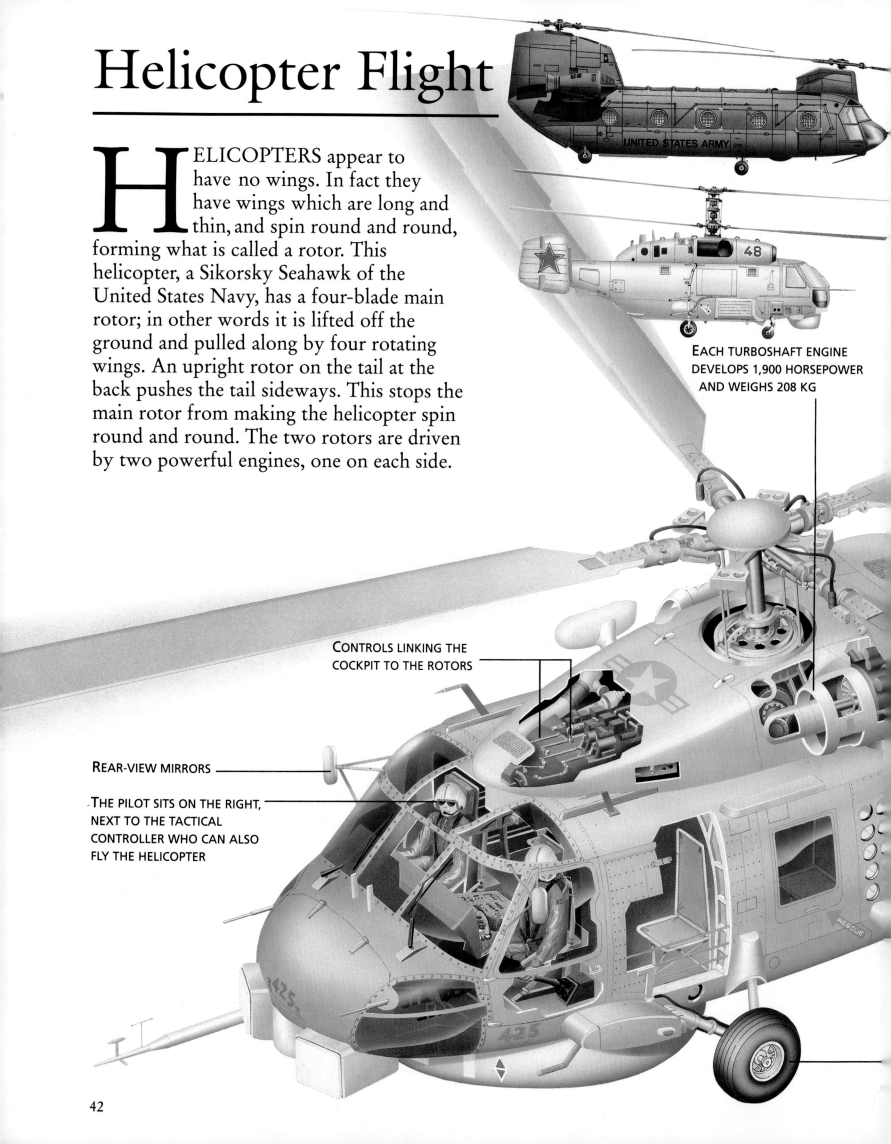

ELICOPTERS appear to have no wings. In fact they have wings which are long and thin, and spin round and round, forming what is called a rotor. This helicopter, a Sikorsky Seahawk of the United States Navy, has a four-blade main rotor; in other words it is lifted off the ground and pulled along by four rotating wings. An upright rotor on the tail at the back pushes the tail sideways. This stops the main rotor from making the helicopter spin round and round. The two rotors are driven by two powerful engines, one on each side.

EACH TURBOSHAFT ENGINE DEVELOPS 1,900 HORSEPOWER AND WEIGHS 208 KG

CONTROLS LINKING THE COCKPIT TO THE ROTORS

REAR-VIEW MIRRORS

THE PILOT SITS ON THE RIGHT, NEXT TO THE TACTICAL CONTROLLER WHO CAN ALSO FLY THE HELICOPTER

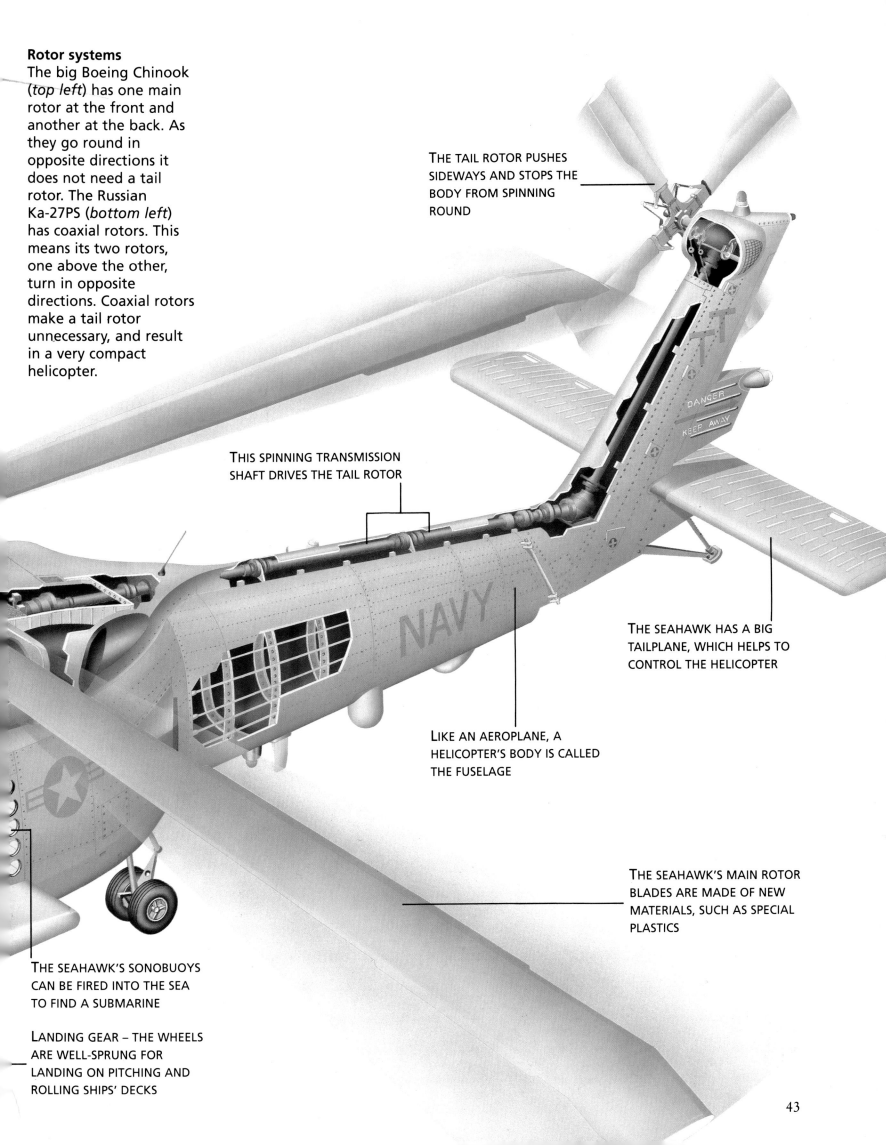

Rotor systems

The big Boeing Chinook (*top left*) has one main rotor at the front and another at the back. As they go round in opposite directions it does not need a tail rotor. The Russian Ka-27PS (*bottom left*) has coaxial rotors. This means its two rotors, one above the other, turn in opposite directions. Coaxial rotors make a tail rotor unnecessary, and result in a very compact helicopter.

THE TAIL ROTOR PUSHES SIDEWAYS AND STOPS THE BODY FROM SPINNING ROUND

THIS SPINNING TRANSMISSION SHAFT DRIVES THE TAIL ROTOR

THE SEAHAWK HAS A BIG TAILPLANE, WHICH HELPS TO CONTROL THE HELICOPTER

LIKE AN AEROPLANE, A HELICOPTER'S BODY IS CALLED THE FUSELAGE

THE SEAHAWK'S MAIN ROTOR BLADES ARE MADE OF NEW MATERIALS, SUCH AS SPECIAL PLASTICS

THE SEAHAWK'S SONOBUOYS CAN BE FIRED INTO THE SEA TO FIND A SUBMARINE

LANDING GEAR – THE WHEELS ARE WELL-SPRUNG FOR LANDING ON PITCHING AND ROLLING SHIPS' DECKS

43

How Rotors Work

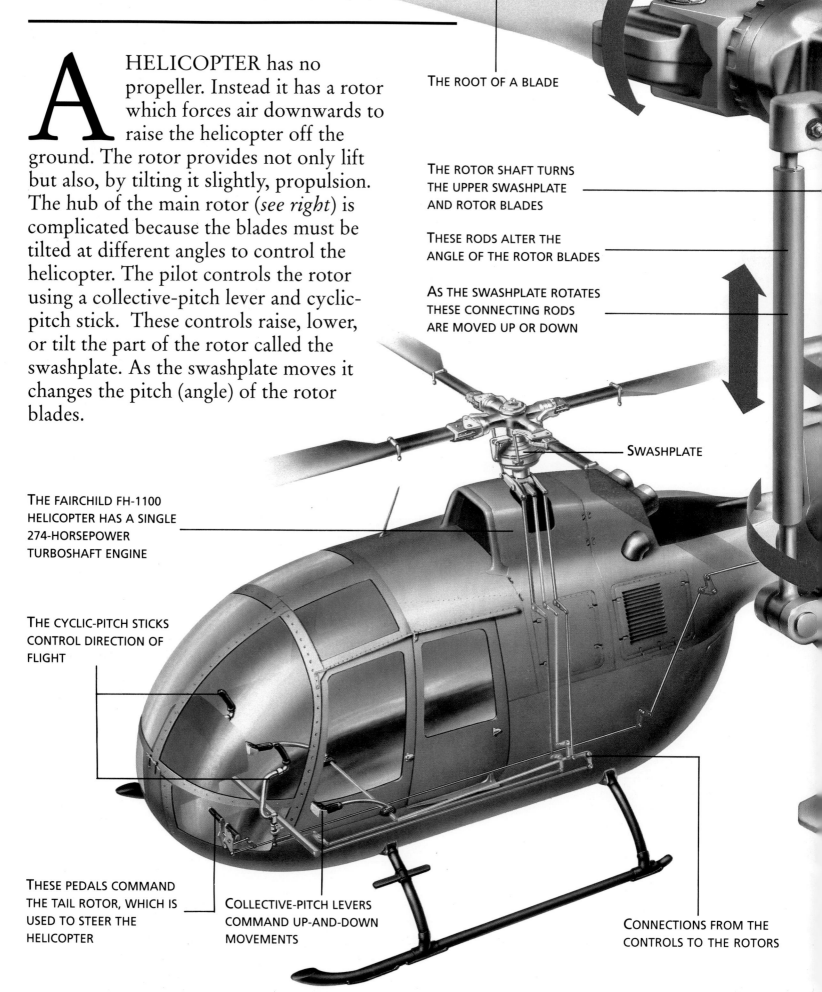

A HELICOPTER has no propeller. Instead it has a rotor which forces air downwards to raise the helicopter off the ground. The rotor provides not only lift but also, by tilting it slightly, propulsion. The hub of the main rotor (*see right*) is complicated because the blades must be tilted at different angles to control the helicopter. The pilot controls the rotor using a collective-pitch lever and cyclic-pitch stick. These controls raise, lower, or tilt the part of the rotor called the swashplate. As the swashplate moves it changes the pitch (angle) of the rotor blades.

THE ROOT OF A BLADE

THE ROTOR SHAFT TURNS THE UPPER SWASHPLATE AND ROTOR BLADES

THESE RODS ALTER THE ANGLE OF THE ROTOR BLADES

AS THE SWASHPLATE ROTATES THESE CONNECTING RODS ARE MOVED UP OR DOWN

SWASHPLATE

THE FAIRCHILD FH-1100 HELICOPTER HAS A SINGLE 274-HORSEPOWER TURBOSHAFT ENGINE

THE CYCLIC-PITCH STICKS CONTROL DIRECTION OF FLIGHT

THESE PEDALS COMMAND THE TAIL ROTOR, WHICH IS USED TO STEER THE HELICOPTER

COLLECTIVE-PITCH LEVERS COMMAND UP-AND-DOWN MOVEMENTS

CONNECTIONS FROM THE CONTROLS TO THE ROTORS

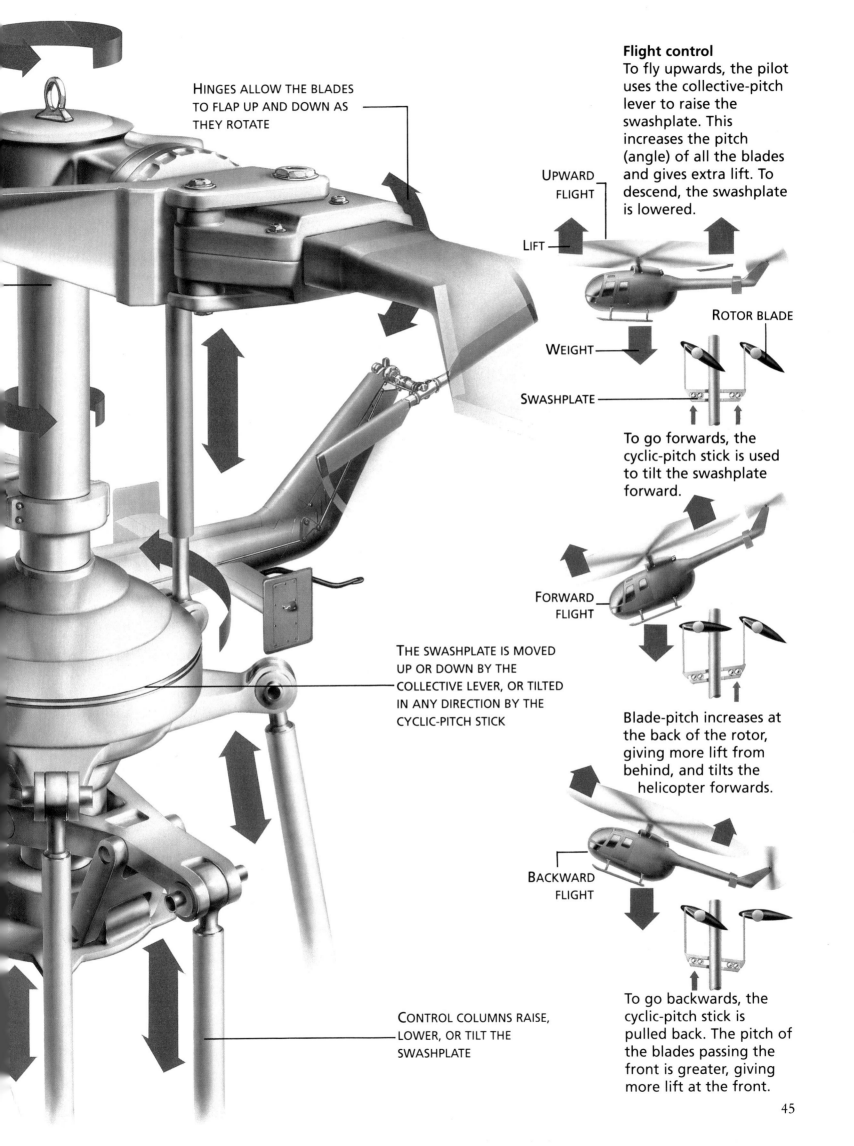

HINGES ALLOW THE BLADES TO FLAP UP AND DOWN AS THEY ROTATE

Flight control
To fly upwards, the pilot uses the collective-pitch lever to raise the swashplate. This increases the pitch (angle) of all the blades and gives extra lift. To descend, the swashplate is lowered.

UPWARD FLIGHT

LIFT

ROTOR BLADE

WEIGHT

SWASHPLATE

To go forwards, the cyclic-pitch stick is used to tilt the swashplate forward.

FORWARD FLIGHT

Blade-pitch increases at the back of the rotor, giving more lift from behind, and tilts the helicopter forwards.

THE SWASHPLATE IS MOVED UP OR DOWN BY THE COLLECTIVE LEVER, OR TILTED IN ANY DIRECTION BY THE CYCLIC-PITCH STICK

BACKWARD FLIGHT

CONTROL COLUMNS RAISE, LOWER, OR TILT THE SWASHPLATE

To go backwards, the cyclic-pitch stick is pulled back. The pitch of the blades passing the front is greater, giving more lift at the front.

45

Index